THE COCKATOO'S LIE

Marion Bloem

TRANSLATED FROM THE DUTCH

BY WANDA BOEKE

WOMEN IN TRANSLATION

Originally published by Uitgeverij De Arbeiderspers as *De Leugen van de Kaketoe.*

Published by arrangement with Uitgeverij De Arbeiderspers.

English translation copyright © 1995 by Wanda Boeke.

Publication of this book was made possible in part with financial support from the National Endowment for the Arts and the Foundation for the Production and Translation of Dutch Literature.

Cover illustration and text design by Clare Conrad.

Library of Congress Cataloging in Publication Data:
Bloem, Marion.
    [Leugen van de kaketoe. English]
    The cockatoo's lie / Marion Bloem: translated from the Dutch by Wanda Boeke.
I. Boeke, Wanda. II. Title.
PT5881.12.L54L4813   1996   839.3'1364—dc20   96-11724
ISBN 1-879679-08-6

First edition, May 1996
Printed in the United States
10 9 8 7 6 5 4 3 2 1

Women in Translation
3131 Western Avenue #410
Seattle WA 98121

Translator's Introduction

In working on the translation of *The Cockatoo's Lie*, it became evident that some words of introduction were necessary in order to create a context for the work for those readers unfamiliar with Indonesian or Dutch-Indonesian history.

Indonesia's thirteen thousand volcanic islands stretch out along the equator some 3182 miles from the Malay peninsula to Papua New Guinea. The country's larger land areas include the island of Sumatra to the west, the larger part of Borneo (Kalimantan) and eastward, the western half of New Guinea (Irian Jaya). The island of interest to this story is Java, about 600 by 120 miles, accommodating nearly two-thirds of the population of Indonesia. Together with Jakarta, the capital, Bandung, Surabaya and Semarang are the major population centers on the island which is traversed east-west by a tall chain of volcanic mountains. The population make-up of Java is largely Malay and Papuan with Chinese, Arabs and others forming minorities. Through centuries of trade and warfare, island populations intermingled. Hindu, Muslim, Christian, Malay and European influences were first felt on the coasts, gradually working their way inland.

Primitive man existed on Java one million years ago. Civilization developed under Indian Hindu influence after the fourth century AD, with Islam making inroads centuries later. The Portuguese entered the picture in 1511, starting with the capture of Malacca on the Malay Peninsula. While retaining East Timor, they lost ground to the Dutch through the latter's Dutch East Indian Company which was set up in then Batavia (later Jakarta) in 1619. This led to The Netherlands resuming control in 1798. During the Napoleonic Wars, a time when The Netherlands was a vassal state of France, the British attacked the Dutch troops and occupied the islands from 1811 until 1813 when Napoleon fell, though they did not turn over control to The Netherlands until 1816. By 1870 the Dutch had established military control in just about all of the Indonesian states, after long decades of brutally quelling continuous rebellions.

One of the remaining free states, Atyeh, located on the northern tip of Sumatra, resisted. The Netherlands officially declared war on this sultanate in 1873. The devout Gayos and Alassers resisted the infidels steadfastly until 1942 when they finally succumbed to over seventy years of mass murder and slavery. It has been claimed that the Dutch could never have succeeded in taking over this area if it had not been for the chain gangs of commandeered island villagers who, among other things, torturously built roads through the rain forest. Early in the twentieth century, nationalist independence movements, some religiously motivated, emerged which were strengthened following Japanese occupation during World War II from 1942 to 1945.

Sukarno, the first president of Indonesia (1945-1967), was the leader of the Partai Nasional Indonesia independence movement which he established in 1927. The Japanese brought the Dutch empire in the archipelago to collapse in 1942. Sukarno outwardly collaborated with the Japanese, who had shown that an Asian nation was not inferior to any European nation, while at the same time working with two nationalist leaders to set up a network of resistance to the Japanese occupation. Sukarno's collaboration gained him a trained, armed military force which he deployed in 1945 against the British who occupied Indonesia after Japanese capitulation. The Americans placed pressure on the Dutch, whose position internationally had weakened considerably, to recognize Sukarno's Republik Indonesia, his control initially over Sumatra and Java and later over the entire archipelago, an agreement that fell apart in 1947 when Dutch troops still in place on the other islands attacked the coasts of Java, Sumatra and Madura using a British blockade of rice shipments as a pretext. The international community was outraged. When, in 1948, the Dutch in a second "policing action" took over the last "republican" region by attacking the city of Yogyakarta, the international community also took action, the US threatening to withhold Marshall aid to The Netherlands. Following a Round Table Conference in The Hague, in which the US played a major role, it was made clear that prewar colonial relationships could no longer exist. Reluctantly the Dutch granted independence to the Republic of the United States of Indonesia in 1949. It was not until 1962, however, after another bloody confrontation between the Indonesians and the Dutch in New Guinea, and after yet another conference in which the US was a major player, that Kalimantan came under Indonesia's control. This ended 336 years of Dutch intervention in the archipelago. Many parallels can be seen between the history of Indonesia and the histories of other Asian countries over the course of these three hundred years of contesting European interests.

Sukarno's at once colorful and corrupt rule, with one-time free elections in 1955, became a dictatorship in 1959. Implicated in an attempted Communist coup in 1965, Sukarno, after three years of struggle, was ousted by General Suharto, who has been the country's president since 1968. Suharto severed links with mainland China and restored relations with the West. Even though Suharto also held one-time free elections in 1971, he actively suppressed left-wing groups. His regime, like Sukarno's, has been widely criticized for being overly repressive and corrupt.

The Netherlands, in line with its general post-colonial attitude, has maintained a helpful and open policy toward Indonesia, including well-nigh automatic citizenship to those Indonesians wishing to live in The Netherlands. Thousands of Indonesians, usually of mixed Dutch-Indonesian background, took advantage of this option after World War II, disturbed by the violence in their homeland during the struggle for independence. Gravitating naturally to form their own communities within Dutch cities, the Indonesian-Dutch population has had a positive impact on Dutch society. One will eat *nasi goreng* in a Dutch home even more often than a traditional pot roast or pea soup. An autumn jacket might very likely be of Ikat weave. Many people around the world are now familiar with Indonesian batiks and have discovered the entrancing charm of gamelan music.

At the core of Marion Bloem's *The Cockatoo's Lie* are two issues of significance to every nation today: the dilution and eventual loss of cultural identity due to assimilation, and the dispelling of a dominant society's xenophobic attitude particularly with regard to race. During the 1950s, as The Netherlands was rebuilding itself in the aftermath of World War II, refugees and others were entering the country in waves. In the 1960s, and especially in the 1970s, there were so many immigrants arriving in The Netherlands from so many damaged and unbalanced nations, including many Americans wanting to avoid active involvement in the Vietnam War, workers from

North Africa, and political refugees from Eastern Europe and South America, that any initial discomfort of opening its doors to Indonesians has given way to a nationalist movement to re-evaluate the country's immigration policy. Nevertheless, the Dutch remain open to difference. When things had settled down in Indonesia, the Dutch rediscovered their former colony as a vacation spot—not an entirely unwelcome initiative as tourism has given a distinct boost to the Indonesian economy.

Translation is not merely the transformation of one word into another, it embodies the movement of one culture into another. I have chosen to maintain Bloem's use of Bahasa Indonesia and Malay terms within the text, providing a glossary, which was not part of the original—presumably because Dutch readers would be familiar with a good number of them. Although I initially entertained the idea of introducing short descriptive or explanatory phrases in the text itself, it became clear in discussion with the author that it was preferable to avoid disruption of the text and so a glossary was decided upon.

Bloem has made the names of some of her characters emblematic, for example the narrator's name, *Meisje*, means Girl. I have chosen to translate some of the names to follow suit. Inevitably there are problems with doing this and I decided to leave, in English spelling, for instance the Dutch *Broos* (my Brose), meaning fragile, as there was no suitable name in English and any concoction on my part would seem just that. Even though *Broos* is not a known name in Dutch, it is not obtrusive in the original text probably because Dutch names often indicate one's geographical origin, the family profession or one's placement within a family.

Inevitably decisions regarding method deeply influence the nature of any given translated work. I have attempted as much as possible to maintain the oral, spontaneous and associative atmosphere of the narrative. Bloem allows several voices to speak in *The Cockatoo's Lie*. There are more than ninety languages in Indonesia. Many people speak different languages, each used in a specific context. Bloem's older Indies (Dutch-Indonesian, see glossary) characters speak an Indies Dutch, not the Dutch of a native speaker from The Netherlands. Indies people in Indonesia would know at least a smattering of Dutch, and it even crept into their own languages. I have tried to imitate this variety of speech with some success, I hope. In addition, the reader will sense that language is a cultural, religious and social tag in this area of the world, and that language can define a people or an individual far more than the color of their skin.

Wanda Boeke
Iowa City, Iowa
January, 1996.

GENEALOGY

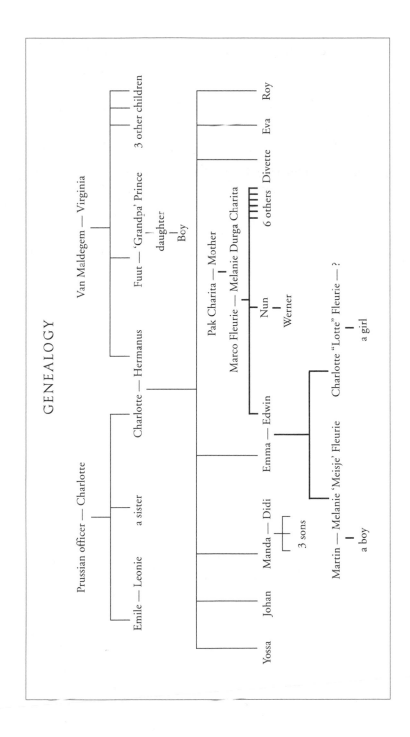

THE COCKATOO'S LIE

I

"My earliest memories are those of the people on the chain gangs. The dirt under their nails, their soft, full, Asian lips in my neck, on my skin, their concerned looks when my pregnant Javanese mother takes me from them and slings me in a batik *slendang*. Their familiar scent, for they smell like fallen mangoes, wet banana leaves, and fresh sweat that makes their dark, naked bodies gleam, still sticks to the hairs of my nostrils. No stench like that of the army fatigues belonging to my Prussian father, musty, mildewed by a mixture of perspiration and monsoon rain, accompanied by the overwhelmingly pungent odor of his heavy boots. Later, when I'm old enough to learn *eins*, *zwei*, *drei*, and so on from him, I have to polish them. They are in the kitchen, where my mother sleeps, along with the other women and us children, on grass mats.

"The memories of my father are from later, from when I can already talk, and he teaches me the multiplication tables from one to ten in his mother tongue.

"First there are the chain gangs. Most of those people don't need chains around their ankles because they hamper walking, you know. They are our porters when my father goes off on an expedition with other soldiers. And they are sweet to me, they carry me. . . . Taking turns, of course.

"I will never forget when they were bound to the posts and beaten. I don't want to see it, but I want to know everything, so I watch with one eye open, one eye shut. I can't talk yet, I'm still little, just a few Javanese words, that's all. Why they are being tortured, I don't know. That's the way it is for one forced to labor, for a slave, for a child, for a woman. Sometimes you get hit and you don't know why. Did something wrong, I suppose."

My own first memory concerns a woman. Not my mother, although she must have been the first to have sheltered me with her body. I was a crybaby. "Always unhappy," said my mother. My father demanded she nurse me the minute I started bawling, so that my mother, who didn't get to sleep much anymore, became weak and I, despite such abundant feeding, remained a delicate baby. I can smell my Aunt Manda, your second daughter, still. As the prettiest daughter, maybe not really the prettiest, but the blondest with the palest skin, who fulfilled the colonial ideal of the Indo-European, she used the most makeup. Fragrant powder, lipstick and perfume that her husband, a non-commissioned officer in the navy, brought back from his distant travels.

I feel the long, fuchsia-colored nails on my skin, her hands hard and cold, I hear her laugh, I see the colors around me. It is dark where she lifts me out of the zinc tub filled with cooled, now tepid water. The first thing that comes back is that I'm slipping, I'm falling—the same fall I still occasionally reenact in my sleep. My feet and legs are cold and wet, and the fall doesn't hurt because she has caught me in time. It all takes less than half a second, maybe. Then, brown tones, that years later I understand must have been batik. The height. She changed me up high. A smell, not of her powder and perfume, but of her home, a remarkable mixture of mothballs, lavender, *terasie*, garlic, bees' wax and bleach—Aunt Manda liked cleaning more than cooking—I can still recall. And that she was probably slower than my mother, or that she had trouble finding my clothes, because I remember lying down for a long time, much longer than usual, without anything on, naked, on my back. A low, wooden ceiling, I remember now. Later we stayed over more often at this aunt's little apartment in the Jordaan, the old working-class neighborhood in the center of Amsterdam, but that first memory is stronger than that of any of my later visits.

Presumably I kicked and cried heartily. Maybe she went to look quickly in the little kitchen for a bottle of her own baby's milk to calm me down. She was awkward, my Aunt Manda; perhaps even her greatest charm, to be awkward in a pleasant way, so that everybody gladly takes all the work off her hands in order to receive her gift of a radiant, grateful smile. I was crazy about her. She was my example. Pale and blonde like her I could never be, because I was the darkest of all your grandchildren, Grandma, and I had a distinctly Asian body, despite my exceptional tallness. But I decided, even as a little girl, not to know everything so well, the way my mother did, or to be so relentlessly severe and intolerant of weakness in others because she herself was so strong and honest. I wanted to be like my aunt: helpless, powerless, but in her very incapacity, strong.

I can see myself lying on nonchalantly draped cloths. In a tiny niche in the cramped upstairs apartment, hidden in a corner where others would very practically have placed a cupboard, my aunt had made a little bench all by herself from scrap wood she had found in the street. I can see myself on this awkwardly high bench, because even when grown-ups sat down their feet didn't reach the floor so my aunt had to set a little stool there as a footrest, lying there, not screaming, not kicking my little bare legs, but waiting, listening to the tram that makes the place shake when it goes by, and enjoying the cool breeze caressing my nakedness.

Actually, I want to write a book, a kind of autobiography, but time and again I start a letter that without thinking I direct to you even though I know that you haven't been able to read letters for a long time already. You'll ask your oldest daughter to read aloud the most important passages in the letter and then you'll have forgotten the opening words before she has even breathed the period at the end of the sentence with a sigh. (Afraid to be lying on my deathbed and discover to my surprise and dismay: "Good Lord, I forgot to live.")

Her bare feet she has placed on the peacock pouf. The ochre-colored sofa with dozens of cushions in the corner of the room is her throne. Her spot, the right-hand corner of the living room sofa, beside the fold-out sewing chest on tall legs with the green volcanoes and blue skies my father painted on it, is sacred, we grandchildren know. We are allowed to warm up her seat beforehand. While she is still busy washing the dishes we nestle ourselves among the many cushions and quibble, "I get to sit next to Grandma."

"No, I do."

"You sat there yesterday."

We fight for a spot beside her, and snuggle against her warm, soft body. One of us gets her lap, letting his or her head lie there until it's bedtime. Another lays his head in her armpit and accepts being deprived of a view of the television. I plunge into the fray only briefly, calculate my chances at leaning my head up against her sturdy arms or feeling her soft thighs under my temple, but in the end, when I see our favorite place to sit pass me by, throw myself at her feet.

"Grandma, can I file your feet?"

From the sewing chest I take the big file which, because of its coarseness, is somewhat like a carrot grater. The different compartments, the various drawers come into view when I pull the latch to the side. My gaze moves greedily over the dozens of colors of thread, the needles of all sizes, elastic in black, in white and off-white wound around a few yellowed postcards of Paris (the Moulin Rouge), big snaps and little snaps on small pieces of cardboard, a chocolate tin full of buttons, three different scissors, of which the asymmetrical one is the most interesting to me, the various pin cushions made of deep yellow batik. . . and red ribbon, silvery thimbles, and a small book with a blue and white batik cover and a red rubber band around it.

The big file, a small nail file and curved nail scissors are in a green box made of stiff paper with a colorful label on it. A girl with bare breasts leaning against a palm tree. The label has been torn on one side and her upper body has been well-blackened with pencil so that the breasts are no longer visible.

Up and down I pass the big file over the thick, yellow calluses on the edges of the soles of her feet and the bottom of her big toe.

"Why don't you go fill an enamel basin with warm water first," says Grandma, "so the calluses can soak and the filing won't be so hard."

Without spilling, hands trembling, my eyes steadily fixed on the sloshing water that levels out again if I stand still for a moment, I bring the heavy basin to the living room and set it down on the pouf. Grandma frees herself from the back of the sofa and the cushions. Proudly I watch the others move over to give her the opportunity to put her feet in the water. The head in her lap and the head in her armpit have to move aside for an instant. There is some pushing and shoving.

"Hey, I'm sitting there."

"No you're not, I was sitting there first."

The reconciliation of just a few minutes before, during which all were content with a shared first place, is over. The boy pulls the girl's hair.

"*Ayó!* Don't quarrel."

One pinches the other on the sly, and the other pulls the first one's hair. The fight is silent. Their angry faces are directed at me.

"*Ayó!* Don't fight." Because she has eyes in the back of her head, too.

She is sitting on the edge of the couch and both her feet are in the basin. One foot is resting on the other. She rubs her hands over her instep and her toes. Meanwhile she watches the television intently. I know each little wrinkle in her face. She doesn't have many. Three near her right eye and two near her left. Two on her forehead when she squints. The painter who came to whitewash the ceiling didn't want to believe that she was almost sixty.

He had seen the thirteen baby pictures on the wall and asked, "Are they all your children?"

"Those are my grandchildren," she had replied.

The man laughed mockingly, "Tell me another one."

She smiled with her lips together.

"Does your mother always make jokes like that?" he asked me.

I looked down at the floor and saw his big pale feet in leather sandals covered with lots of white speckles so the brown leather was barely visible.

"A grandmother like that I'd like to have, too," the man had said.

And then I looked up politely at his scary whitewashed face. He winked first at me and then at Grandma, who acted like she didn't notice anything and walked off toward the kitchen.

While she is soaking her feet, I walk over to the linen closet in the living room. On the inside of the door dozens of pictures of movie stars and of members of the royal family have been tacked up. Some of them have yellowed. A few color photographs have been hung among them recently. Romy Schneider wearing a little crown is displayed beside a torn one of the Dutch queen mother, Wilhelmina. A yellowed piece of tape has pressed her short neck even further into her high-collared dress. From the pile I grab a thin white cotton cloth for drying Grandma's feet and sniff at it before shutting the closet again. (Grandma's clean wash smells like my mother's. At my aunts' the towels smell different, and the sheets just like home. I like the difference, but my pillow case always has to smell a bit sweet.)

The footbath is poured out over the many geraniums by the window. Aunt Yossa, the oldest of my mother's sisters, who lives with her parents, and who at thirty barely reaches my shoulder, helps me, even though I snap at her, "I can do it all by myself. . . ." With my back toward the television, I sit on a wooden lilac-colored stool. The tips of my fingers caress Grandma's toes. Her toes are steps, different than mine where the second toe tries to be longer than the big one. "You're jealous," my father had said pointing at my toes, "you got them from me."

The little toe has a thin strip of hard callus, taut and tight like the rim of a cookie tin. I work on it with the small file. The foot I'm filing lies warm on top of my thigh. Sometimes the sole of her foot touches my stomach. Her other foot rests between the two bluish purple peacocks. The pouf is our toy. We roll on it around the living room, down the hall, in the dining room under the big round table until Grandma wants to sit on her throne. Then we hurry as fast as we can to slip the pouf under her feet just in time.

Before there was a television, she liked to tell stories.

"What kind of expeditions were they?"

"To protect the plantations. I don't know exactly. That's the way it is back then."

"But you lived on Sumatra, didn't you?"

"Yes, but we keep moving around That's the way it is back then."

"Was there a war, Grandma?"

"Maybe. . . I think so."

"Which one? The Atyeh War?"

"Oh, I don't know, I can't keep track of those things, child. All the time, though, all those men together, fighting all the time."

(Grandma, from the moment I left my mother's belly, I've cared too much for the male sex.)

Instead of a book, I'll write a letter. Sentences that I want to entrust in confidence to paper because I am convinced that the reader will cherish them like I do. Each page after reading will be carefully folded back up on the fold I pressed into it after writing. The envelope will protect it from dust and envious eyes. The pages will be kept in sequence in an old shoe box, or preferably even a small chest bought at a flea market somewhere. With care a new lock will be mounted on the old box so that the secrets I have laid bare in my letter won't become public knowledge.

. . .

She smiles, her gaze fixed on infinity as she sings rather than says, "*Eins mal drei macht drei, zwei mal drei macht sechs, drei mal drei macht neun. . . .*"

To whom should I write the letter? To my girl friend, whom I've already been updating on my daily affairs for fifteen years? There was a time that we wrote each other like intimate lovers every day. We exchanged every detail with each other. She wrote how she had fixed potatoes for the evening meal. Cooked briefly, first, then sliced up and fried in butter with onions and garlic. How the oldest of her three children would lick his fingers while he ate and beam, "Mamma, you're the best cook in the whole world."

I described to her the content of the letter from my lover in Los Angeles, sent a snapshot of my new acquaintance in Budapest, described how I missed the date with the Italian pianist in Copenhagen and so got to know a Norwegian pilot there, and recited the poem from my secret ex-love in Yogyakarta. Beside her own sometimes slightly dull existence, she said, she was able to experience along with me, by means of my letters, the excitement that often seemed to plague me. I found peace of mind in her descriptions of the daily goings-on and chuckled at the disarming conversations she had with her small children.

Since more harmony has come into my life, so that my days are a little more monotonous, the energy to write up all the day's phone conversations, encounters and letters eludes me. And now that she has started working, now the children are older, and now that even she occasionally meets a man with whom she shares more than with her husband, she in turn can't find enough time to keep me abreast of all the details of her daily life.

My letters to this friend would not, despite the faithfulness with which I recounted all the high points of my existence, be a true picture of that time in my life. I know so well what's missing.

A letter to my slightly older and only sister is closer to the style and content I have in mind. Our shared childhood, the similarities between us, but particularly the differences, would be occasion to bring up all kinds of memories that made me into who I am now. But then again because of our shared childhood, such a letter, in the form of a book, would induce anxiety in a third reader. An outside reader might feel shut out, not understand our language and feel threatened by the bond that would reveal itself in style and content.

A letter to my mother would entail the required distance, but would be filled with admissions of guilt, and who benefits from a public confession?

A letter to the father of my son would entail the same problem. I would feel shame for past behavior for which I had never felt shame before, a shame which deep in my heart, I believe isn't necessary.

My son, my father, my brothers. . . . Senseless letters. They wouldn't appreciate my disclosures.

A letter to myself would be straightforward; am I not the only person, in fact, with this intense need to read such a letter?

Every letter is a coming to terms with an identification, with moralism, with guilt, with history.

Instead of life now, I would like to describe my life up until now as a guideline for the future. As a balance sheet of joys and sorrows whose totals I can carry forward. The importance lies in all the details, or should I say all the details of the contacts and confrontations with the many women around me from the moment of my birth, and perhaps even from long before that, that made me into who I am now.

But for the time being I am searching for words. The beginning does not lie in my memory, the beginning lies where I fantasize it.

Fabrications are what I want to write. I want to explain who I am, and why at forty years of age I am afraid to live. I want to try to understand who I am. No autobiography to protect myself, an autobiography to forget myself. To get caught up in longing and to discover why, time after time, I take another breath while I no longer savor the air.

Too bad you weren't here yesterday. Although I promised to pick you up so that you could be at my fortieth birthday party, I decided at the last minute not to stop by. The reason was that my love (or should I say ex-love)—no, not my husband, Grandma, he had to go to the supermarket, the liquor store and the bakery to get things for the party—called me in the morning to say that he would really prefer not to come. And this resulted in two hours of talking and crying, but mostly saying nothing, each of us pressing the receiver in our hand against our left ear, so it got too late to pick you and Auntie up from the retirement residence before the first guests arrived.

A few months ago we celebrated your ninetieth birthday, that was the last time that I saw you.

You no longer remember that there was going to be a party

and you have forgotten that you were going to come and forgotten that you unfortunately didn't come to my party. Aunt Yossa said that yesterday you must have asked twenty times, "Aren't we supposed to go out dancing today?"

Auntie cancelled the weekly dance evening with the other Indies seniors because you were coming to my party. You didn't know about that, either. Three years ago my parents celebrated forty years of marriage. You danced all night long, and Aunt Yossa was afraid that it would be too much, so she asked would the ladies and gents leave you be for fifteen minutes or so. The party was winding down, the hall was getting emptier. "Shall I take you home?" one of my cousins asked, and your voice sounded indignant, "How can that be! So soon? I haven't danced at all yet."

Every day you ask your oldest daughter at least a dozen times if the two of you will be going out today. And regardless of the answer, fifteen miutes or an hour later you'll ask again.

"We're going to Meisje's, she's turning forty today."

"Is she?"

"Remember how she used to dance on the table, one hand on her stomach and the other above her head, and how she swayed her hips."

Aunt Yossa is happy when she hears you say for the sixth time that day, "So old already? How's that possible?" This, rather than the question, "Meisje? Who's that again?"

It was too late to organize transportation for your Indies group. But Aunt Yossa didn't let on that she was disappointed. Her voice sounded warm.

"Doesn't matter, better luck next time, we aren't dead yet."

The fifty years that lie between you and me were there yesterday evening at my party in the form of Helena, a Dutch acquaintance visiting me. She dyes her short curly hair red, but her eyebrows are gray, just like her long eyelashes, and that lends her eyes something mischievous. Her mouth is, however, narrow and tight, now more than it used to be, with hard lines at the corners and little furrows around her upper lip. She hasn't menstruated in five months, she says, and feels "fantastic."

"Nothing's bothering me, everything's fine, except my body has changed. There is one thing that's a pity, and that is. . . I notice on the street and at parties that the young people shut me out. No flirtatious glances on café terraces anymore. And they forget you at conferences and festivals after a spontaneous decision to go grab a beer somewhere. I'm the one who has to pay attention and run after them, otherwise I'll suddenly be left behind all by myself."

It has been a year or two since I last saw her. Her body had always been on the heavy side. Her breasts, voluminous, stuck straight out, defiantly, provocatively, but now they appear to have become a single unit with stomach and backside.

"Sex is different," she says. She looks serious. Her green eyes look gray. "You aren't as hot as you used to be, things don't happen naturally anymore."

I don't believe her, Grandma.

Your smile is still like the slit in the curtain through which the actors secretly watch the public pouring in before the performance starts. The promise of the spectacle without giving away anything about the upcoming show. You were fifty-five, I think, when I stared at your breasts from behind my pillow and trembled with excitement. The folds between your neck and bosom intrigued me. The skin moved as you draped your full-length slip, gracefully removed over your head, carefully over a chair so the cotton fabric wouldn't wrinkle. At least, I think I was five years old when I spied on you out of the corners of my eyes and kept myself awake all evening to see, when you undressed for bed, your café au lait breasts pop out of your bra of an almost identical color.

I could describe my life from the male point of view. I would start with my father, I think, or with my grandfather, or with my first infatuation, at three years of age, or with the loves I recognized as loves only after the fact: the cousins who tickled me behind the curtain of Grandma's foldaway bed, or pressed me up against the boxes of old newspapers in an intimate embrace behind the kitchen door, the blond, sturdily built boy with the green eyes in kindergarten, big hands, soft mouth, that showered me with kisses, but who cursed me out as dirty brown chink shit if I didn't do what he said. Through the women in my immediate surroundings who were my ideals, my examples of how things were, weren't and really weren't supposed to be done, I can show my evolution from girl to flower and, I fear, to dried flower.

"Grandma, tell us again about before."
"Oh. . . before is past."

Your history, and so my history, is unwritten. My parents existed neither in literature nor in textbooks. Everything I know about their past they told me only after I had begged and begged them to talk about what life was like before.

Bewilderment. In order to forget him—his loud laughter, his hands on my neck, his patting my thigh, my shoulder or my arm, the playful way he pinched my sleeping nipples in passing so that they became proudly erect reminded of his hungry mouth—I went to a city that was unfamiliar to me in a country of whose existence I was previously unaware. A young man I met there, not just by chance, because it seemed to be love that drew us together, of about my son's age, with a hungry look in his eye, sensual lips, brown-green eyes and pitch black eyelashes, short curved eyebrows and the body of a fearful deer, taught me how to cup a bumblebee in my hands without hurting the creature and without being scared. "Listen to the even way it buzzes. If you listen well, you'll know when to let it go again."

He showed me the summer after a frosty spring. Because I saw our being together as a blossom that fades and falls to make way for ripe apples, less pale but with more weight, he would snap at me, his face a scream, panic in his eyes, "You don't live, you're just busy writing your autobiography."

He was a poet, he said, and his poetry, already published in literary journals by the time he was eighteen, had nothing to do with his life. He prided himself in that, that he didn't use what he gleaned from life as fodder for his talent. "My ambition is to derive the most ecstasy possible out of life," he said, "I wrote my best poems when I was unhappy, when I was apathetic. Better to live than write poetry." And that's what he demanded of me. His passion, he said, he saw answered in my eyes, but my words belied the look there. I could do nothing but admit, "You're right. I used to be like you, but now only those experiences that are fascinating to read are worth living, to me."

He searched for words to insult me. As if he felt triumphant at my admission, he repeated, "You don't live to live, you live to write about it."

"I'm almost forty," I said pedantically, coolly, as if we hadn't

17

already kissed away age and experience in our intimate entwining, "and you haven't been wandering the earth even half the time I have. You don't understand that I don't want to repeat anything in my life, that I'm only looking for those experiences that I haven't recognized yet, that are new, that stimulate me, that, as a matter of fact, remind me of my ambition to write." We were shouting. Me. Him. Me. Him. In turns. And, at the same time, which you detest.

The torrent of his words, his attempts to put his arms around me, hold me close, despite my protests, his childishly desperate face, I took seriously. Each sentence was weighed, until I knew that the hopeless look on his face was what I and not he should be feeling, because I'm the bumblebee.

I'm not ashamed, Grandma, that for me the greatest thrill is to live in order to write about it. Or should I say that I only feel that I'm alive when I can write about it? But that isn't it either.

The discovery, while writing, of existing on a higher level than that of action, than words, and to touch the unutterable through the simple coupling of searching sentences, is what makes me aware that I'm alive.

(Yesterday my cockatoo, whom I fed much too late because I'd been on the phone for so long, spoke for the first time.)

II

"My illness is my punishment. I regret my wrongdoing, but my flesh is weak, you know."

As we stomp the snow off our shoes, the smell of songbird seed already greets us. The blue veins that seem to lie on top of my Grandpa's pale skin protrude when he picks up my two-year-old son and holds him tight.

"*Adú!* You've gotten heavy, my word, built like a *belanda*."

We have come by special request. It is exceptional. He never asks. His eyes seem sunken deeper than ever in their sockets. He looks like a delicate bird, a bantam plucked bald; his nose, sharp and oversized for an Indonesian's, sticks out gauntly like a beak.

"You both smell of the outdoors." He rubs his nose and hollow cheeks and wipes the cold we brought in off his face.

"They've gone to the market, your grandmother pulling your Aunt Yossa in the sleigh. Dangerous, for sure, it's so slick, but you know that aunt of yours, bull-headed as she is, she wants to go out. . . ."

"I saw their tracks," I say.

"Peep, peep," says the boy. He is pointing at the small cage in the hallway and wanders toward the next cage in the dining room. "More peep peep." And then, with squeals of joy, he runs to the third, the fourth, "More peep peep!"

The boy, their first great-grandchild, has his own rituals. I have mine. On a stool behind the kitchen door there is still the pale green fruit crate with all the paper bags from the store that my Grandma has smoothed flat after use, refolded in their creases and saved. Brown with brown. White with white. And then the small pile of clear ones. We used to help her fold them. The plastic bags would get washed and pinned onto the lace curtain of the balcony door with clothes pegs. There is soup on the gas burner, as always. I lift the lid of the saucepan and sniff the slightly sour aroma of the leftovers that have been worked into it. The soup makes me a child. (Back then, when he was still going to the office, he kept his aviary downstairs in the storage unit of the postwar apartment and would bring the birds upstairs in little bamboo cages only when it froze. The bulbul in the kitchen, his favorite songbird, roamed the house with or without its cage. The Indonesian lark and a few magnificent finches he would keep in the dining room, in the corner beside the bathroom door. But now there are cages everywhere in their apartment.)

Near the gold-colored cage that stands in the tiny kitchen blocking the way to the balcony, the boy stands still; he looks full of anticipation at the slight man who, as always, opens the little door, letting the bulbul walk on his hand to set it down on the boy's shoulder.

The little creature pecks at his neck. The boy, whose cheeks are already glowing from the tropical temperature of the rooms, shivers. His expression reflects pleasure as well as fear. First, there is a look of delight in his eyes, then the shiver comes and the little mouth that grimaces. The knotted, wrinkly hands take the bird from his neck just in time. Cheerfully the boy toddles on, pointing at the biggest cage, "More peep peep," his high voice bright.

He takes five caps out of the closet and two from the coatrack. One by one he fits them on the child's head. His shrunken little bird's head is the same size as the child's, who with respect lets him place first one cap then another on his blond curls. "Here." All seven caps he has piled up, and that's how he sets the pile down on the pouf in front of the boy. "All for you."

Then he slowly gets up, walks over to the coatrack again with small slow steps and shows us a brown suede cap trimmed with fur that's much too big and has ear flaps that can be tied under the chin through a buckle. Only his nose pokes out; for the rest, nothing of his head is visible.

"I still have this one for if I have to go to the specialist. Besides that I won't be going out anymore anyway. I'm only going to tell you because you went to school. But I've got. . . ." At this point he forms the letter C with his fingers. "I'm being punished for my weakness."

We walked on his back. One by one. All together. We were allowed to jump up and down. "Go on, harder," he would say. He had big black spots on his back. Some were flat, some were little dark mounds on his pale skin. There were big ones and very little ones.

"What are those, Grandpa?"

"I got those from my mother. When I was born."

His mother was beautiful, had heavy straight eyebrows and a stern look on her face. In the fancy picture above the television she seems to want to hide her sensual mouth away by clamping her lips between her teeth. It makes her chin look masculine, appearing to protrude slightly because of the clenched lips. But in one of the albums there is also a blurry picture of his mother in which the sorrowful widow doesn't realize that she is being photographed. This photo betrays the full, provocative lips, the feminine jawline that becomes mysterious because of the sad, staring eyes. The photo was taken right after the death of her husband. Someone took a picture of the five children the way they were standing in a row in their white shifts in the yard, still unaware of the death of their father whom they had hardly seen anyway. The still young mother was sitting on the porch swing in a daze, probably worrying about her own future and that of her children because of his many debts. She had been left with four daughters and a son. Her husband had been a well-to-do Fleming who had emigrated to Indonesia, leaving the country of his birth because the wife his parents had selected for him wasn't to his liking. Without the social control of his family he couldn't resist colonial society. He gambled away his money and, without trying to keep it a secret, dated many Indies women whom he generously rewarded with jewelry for the attentions they paid him. He was a welcome guest in the nearby opium den where, out of pity, he let destitute Chinese smoke with him at his expense.

Her father, a Dutch man from Rotterdam who, while an officer in the colonial army, had fallen in love with the daughter of a Madurese prince, gave her the name Virginia, but her Madurese mother always called her Nilly, so her real name wasn't used anymore after that. At the death of her Flemish husband she insisted that everybody call her Virginia again.

Without a father, since he had lost his life in one of the uprisings on Sumatra against the colonial government, and without a mother, since she had died of grief shortly after the death of her husband, Virginia lived with two fears: that her children would end up on the fringe of the *kampong*, and that her reputation as an Indies woman might be questioned in some way. No man, not even a relative, was now allowed to enter her house without being accompanied by a woman. Worried that her children would have their father's character, she brandished the cane. She asked for God's support and that of the priests of the Roman Catholic parish, forced the children to go to mass first thing every morning before school, went with them twice a week to benediction, prayed to all the saints she knew by name, and had her little altar at home, starting with the statue of Maria and the baby Jesus reaching out his helping hand to the world, and later including the additions of the Sacred Heart, a large cross and the statues of the holy Martin, the holy Theresa and the holy Anthony. Every night before going to bed the widow and her five children would kneel on their bare knees on the tile floor and pray for half an hour, no Hail Marys or Our Fathers, but an improvised prayer made up by Virginia who begged God, Maria and the saints, according to the events of the day, to make virtuous, diligent believers of her children so they wouldn't lose their way and would be able to resist all the temptations in life.

Your Javanese mother, shanghaied along with many other Javanese girls from the poor villages of East Java to service in all ways the European soldiers defending the colony on Sumatra from rebels, was very different from your mother-in-law, who probably thought no girl was good enough for her only son. I dreaded your Prussian father not only because of the photograph of him with his fat stomach, the standing collar of his uniform buttoned all the way up, half of a cigar sticking out of the corner of his mouth, his bald swollen head with the big gray curly mustache, but because of what you said about your mother who would beg for mercy and for her *"surat lepas"* when he was once again dragging her through the barracks by her hair, or beating her with his belt. I hoped that Europeans never roamed the house as ghosts and I asked my Aunt Yossa for confirmation, "Only dead Indonesians turn into ghosts, right Auntie. . . ?" Being a simple farmer's son, as he referred to himself, your father had probably also been kidnapped, or in any case picked up by dockyard agents, so-called "farmer catchers," because of the European agricultural crisis, and probably had no idea in what kind of war he was going to end up.

"Why did your German father go to Indonesia?"

"I don't know, maybe he had a falling out, or there was too little money."

"What's a *surat lepas*, Grandma?"

"Oh, a kind of letter of discharge, but I don't know exactly though, you know, except that only with such a letter can she leave him, because she is his property after all."

The story at which your eyes started sparkling was the chink to heaven. You don't reminisce anymore, because before is past, and you've forgotten everything. But, if I ask, "Grandma, tell me about the blonde lady and the *dokar*," the sparkle returns to your eyes.

"I'm still little. Three years old, maybe four, but I don't think so, because I'm far under school age. Now and then a *dokar* comes up to the door, a horse and a little carriage with a blonde Dutch lady in it. Sometimes she doesn't come, then the servant will have been sent to pick me up with the horse and carriage. I have to go play with her little boy. She has a son my age. Maybe I was a sweet child, or she thinks I'm nice, or she wants a daughter too. One day she comes with the *dokar* and steps inside. I can still see her standing there. Light shines in behind her as she is standing in the kitchen. One of those communal kitchens where all the women cook for their menfolk. My mother already has three children by then. My little brother Emile is at her breast, just born. She is big, that lady, and she gives my mother a lot of money, because all the other women are shocked.

"My mother says, 'No, how can I go and sell her? I'm not some kind of rabbit that goes and sells her children off.'

"And then I can't go with her. I have to stay with my mother. That's just how it is."

I wanted to start my autobiography with you.

Grandpa had to play chess to be able to marry you. Not with the help of sheets knotted together, no courtly kidnapping, but with chess pieces on a board. Hermanus van Maldegem, a white Indo-European, both eyes twinkling in a striking face, with a slender but athletic body, had seen the gorgeous seventeen-year-old Charlotte sitting among the other girls at the main switchboard office of which he would shortly be appointed director. He had his mother's proud, straight back, a brown eye from her and a green eye from his father, the diligence of his mother and the loquaciousness of his father. Not only with his pale skin color and his handsome appearance did he charm the ladies, but also with his sense of humor. Just like his father he liked women: young, old, brown, blonde, fat or thin. There was a light blonde, childless Frisian woman, who had had to manage for months without her officer husband since he had gone to one of the islands to quell a rebellion, through whom he lost his virginity when he was fourteen. He had been bidden to come to her home after she had seen him on the tennis court, where he had beaten his older opponent 6-0, and she had let his mother know that she would be pleased to take tennis lessons from him to stave off the boredom. He arrived at the officer's home, as had been agreed, in his tennis whites with two rackets. The houseboy didn't ask him to take a seat on the front porch, but led him to the back gallery, where the servant offered him black Tobruk-style coffee and some sweet tidbits. Two fat cats jumped on his lap one at a time. He had a dislike for cats, thought them murderers, since even at that time he was keeping birds and bantams. He shoved them brusquely from his lap and one of the cats scratched his thigh with her claws. The coffee was still too hot to drink when the maid came to say that madam was waiting for him. He had found it a bit strange that she had let him come during the siesta and understood it even less when she called him inside. He was certain that they would be going together by horse and carriage to the tennis court and he was already looking forward to his friends seeing him with her in the carriage. The rackets stayed behind on the chair as the maid preceded him with a slight bow to the farthestmost corner of the back gallery. The door to the room was open, but the heavy double curtains were shut. He knocked on the window. There was no response. He knocked again, and again.

"Come in, Mannie." Her voice sounded husky.

He drew the curtain aside, saw nothing, was afraid of stumbling, and groped around in the darkness. It was hot and close in the little room. He smelled her body nearby. The pungent scent of her body, like that of cats, did not appeal to him. As he blinked his eyes to get used to the darkness, he could feel her sweaty fingers undoing the top button of his tennis shorts. Her wet fingers, and shortly thereafter her wet tongue, made him unsteady on his feet. He fell or was pulled down onto the tile floor that felt cold to his legs and buttocks. He still had his tennis shirt on when, not ashamed in front of the servants, he heard himself cry out with pleasure.

Hermanus was twenty, and thought it was getting to be

time, with the prospect of that job, as he put it "to build a nest instead of flying around hither and thither, always scared of catching some disease or other." Charlotte was still a virgin, he was certain of that, so he did not need to fear getting syphilis from her. He inquired after her address, planted friends about to find out more about her parents, and one day, despite the humid heat of the wet monsoon, went there wearing a white high-collared button-up jacket over his shirt. Droplets of sweat beaded up on his forehead when a Javanese woman had him sit on the front porch among the bougainvillea, and without asking about the purpose of his visit, she vanished into the house again. A moment later a stocky, sturdily-built man appeared, his mustache stiffly erect like cheerful curtains in front of his cheeks, his stern eyes the color of water, his head bald. The man stood in front of him, legs akimbo, and said with a heavy German accent, "I've already set up the pieces."

"'*Ganz gewiss, ganz gewiss*,' I can still hear him say. My father learned from us children how to speak Dutch. Just imagine, though, a German father with a Javanese wife, how is it possible? Oh well, it's their life. . . . You ask yourself how that is possible, anyhow, a German father and a Javanese mother. . . ." You shake your head. "*Adú!* So what do children want to learn, anyway?"

That evening he had not caught a single glimpse of Charlotte, nor had he dared to speak of her. Her father did not say a word during the game, coughed a lot, and when he was caught in a difficult position, got stuck in a well-nigh asthmatic coughing fit. A small, dark girl—Hermanus suspected she was Charlotte's youngest sister—fanned cool air towards her father.

When her small hand tired and the fanning flagged, he would growl like a malcontent dog, at which the girl would immediately pick up the pace again. The child spied on him, saw Hermanus out of the corner of her eye, but if he caught her at it, she would quickly glance at the broken fan in the ceiling. When he was in check mate, the old man fell silent, lit a cigar and disappeared into the other room. After ten minutes he still had not returned, but then a fourteen-year-old boy appeared, with pale skin, not as pale as his father's or his own, nor was he as dark as Charlotte or the little girl. The boy was unmistakably a brother because he had the same nose, the same mischievous eyes, and the same provocative mouth. "You may return tomorrow for a rematch."

By the next morning, when he made inquiries of his friends about Charlotte's father, he had figured out the misunderstanding that had taken place. Her father had been promised an opponent long before by an acquaintance, but the young man still had not shown up. That very afternoon Hermanus procured the name and address of the chess player and offered the young man a week's wages if he would stay out of the picture. The following evenings he managed to lose to the old man. Now and again he caught sight of Charlotte, with whom he had still not exchanged a word, when she slipped through the room to get plates from the cabinet.

Only after many months, after she had often disrupted the quiet of the room with her soft tread and when the old man had already often noticed that his opponent couldn't keep his eyes off his oldest daughter, did he introduce him to her.

"Haven't I seen you before at the switchboard office?" asked Hermanus sanctimoniously.

Charlotte lowered her eyes. For months she had been teased by the girls in her department about this dashing young man who with his gaze tried to tear off the silver brooch that kept her white lace blouse shut tight.

At the staff evening party, where from the moment the orchestra struck up through to the final number, she had glided over the dance floor, one gentleman after another asking her to dance, he had stood and watched her, unmoving, from the sidelines. She had dreamed many times of dancing the tango or the Viennese waltz in his arms. The older girls said that he, being the best dancer at the office, had never before allowed a single dance to pass him by, and that there was no doubt that he had more than a passing fancy for her.

In fact, you were secretly engaged to someone of Portuguese background. He had given you a gold ring after you had permitted him to kiss you on your closed lips following a party at the tennis club. All the girls were in love with this dark man with the straight nose and the flashing eyes who was known as "the gangster" because of his cocky way of walking and his style of dressing, recalling those black and white movies shown at the nearby movie house. You had heard from your girl friends that your secret fiancé regularly went on his motorcycle to visit a family whose three daughters had questionable reputations. When you asked him about this, he shrugged his shoulders and mumbled sweet phrases in English or Portuguese, caressed your fingers and your arms up to your elbows. (You told me a couple of times about this secret fiancé. I greedily sucked up your words like melted Javanese sugar from the warm little *kelepon* with the flip top.)

One day you went to his house, far from your work and far from your parents' home. He was taken aback by your unexpected visit. You had never been there before, and he had never invited you to his house. In the door stood a Javanese lady, barefoot, dressed in a sarong and *kebaya*, just like your mother, her gray-black hair in a bun in her neck, who welcomed you in Malaysian and indicated a chair where you could wait for your fiancé.

He sent the Javanese woman away. Rudely, half in Malaysian, half in Javanese.

"Who is that woman?"

"That's a distant aunt of mine who helps us in the house."

"Why are you lying to me, she isn't your aunt, she's your mother. Are you ashamed of her? I have a Javanese mother, too, don't I?"

You gave him back the ring and felt relieved.

Patiently you waited for Hermanus to have the courage to speak to you, and you giggled with your girl friends about how he came over every evening to play chess with your father, even though he had never spoken to you at the office. However, now that he was shaking your hand for the first time, you felt the blood rush to your head.

You fled the room and heard your father say to him, "She is still a virgin. And she is diligent. If you like, you might take her to the movies some time. And she likes to dance. Or do you play tennis?"

(These are the stories with which I grew up, that made me and betrayed me.)

Aunt Manda likewise let herself be won through her father. Because she was blonde, and therefore grew up with the least concern, she maintained her engaging childlike smile, despite her camp years which were more threatening to her than to my mother or her other sisters just because of the fact that the Japanese had an appetite for pale, blonde girls. As a child she was already dressing with a modest elegance that had also been her grandmother Virginia's style. It seemed as if Virginia van

Maldegem had been fighting her own allure. In spite of her attempts to be puritanical and strait-laced, she had been cursed with a certain way of moving, talking and laughing which charmed not only men, but women as well. The way she rolled her dark Van Nelle tobacco into cigarettes, even the way she burned the finely ground herbs, prescribed by her doctor to prevent asthma attacks, in a small saucer, and the teasingly hesitant way in which she sniffed the smoke aroused desire.

Already when she was a little girl, Manda exercised the same power of attraction over people, and even her strict father, the ambitious van Maldegem, was loath to punish her when she came home from school with failing grades. Just as with the other children, he let either his hand or the cane forcefully strike her legs for every grade lower than a C, but only with Manda was it, in retrospect, as if he had struck himself.

Yossa, as the oldest daughter, with her sunny mischievous character, was already a magnet for those nearest her. Virginia enjoyed showing up at receptions and parties with the girl who, because of her relatively large but beautiful head and her slight, somewhat disabled body, was so endearing. The dwarf child was a pleasant distraction if the men's overtures became a little too enthusiastic, and with this cheerful grandchild at her side she never had to fear that she wouldn't be able to resist the various temptations. Hermanus and Charlotte's second child, Johan, a bright boy who could already read at the age of four, play tennis at six, and who taught himself guitar by inquiring here and there about guitar chords, made friends easily not only because he was sociably adept, but also because there were so many fun sisters running around his house. Johan, a year younger than Yossa and two years older than Manda, was surrounded by boys who wanted to rank foremost in Manda's good graces.

Manda was ten years old when they started trying to

wheedle a promise from her regarding the future. Her answer was always the same disarming smile.

Didi seemed to ignore Manda. He was eighteen and Manda was ten when he first walked onto the van Maldegems' front lawn, inquiring after Mr. Hermanus van Maldegem.

"I heard you kept chickens and birds, and I thought you might want to start flying pigeons. I've got seven carrier pigeons here."

He set the box down on the porch.

"What am I supposed to do with pigeons?" asked van Maldegem. "As the head of the telegraph service, I have more than enough to do with that nonsense." But the corners of his mouth belied interest. Carefully he opened the box, and when he saw those fourteen dark little eyes, he acknowledged defeat.

You said, "Grandpa already has so many hobbies." You detested his frequent trips with his songbirds to participate in bird shows in other cities, even though he always came home with a prize. For several months already you had hidden his soccer things because you didn't want him going off again.

"Lotte, Lotte," he would call, "have you seen my soccer gear anywhere?"

You acted as if you hadn't heard him. He would search the entire house, while you laughed to yourself, until it was too late for him to take part in the match, and then you would feel guilty and, without being noticed, put his sports clothes back again. But a week later you couldn't help doing it again.

You would have loved to play tennis or dance together every day, but after what happened once, you didn't much like to see him go out the door by himself. You were afraid the carrier pigeons would make him stay away from home, but the opposite proved to be the case. The badminton court that

Grandpa had laid out in the back yard was lined by dovecotes.

Didi became his best friend. If he had to go out of town, Didi would take care of the pigeons. Manda wasn't used to men not paying her any attention, and once when her father had taken his bulbul to Yogyakarta and Didi, who had already been a son of the house for a year, had been given one of the rooms on the back gallery as a permanent guest residence, she urged Emma, my mother, to give the pigeons a paint bath on the sly so that Didi would have a run-in with my father. While Didi was taking his siesta, Manda and Emma snuck out of their room and dipped dozens of pigeons in the colors red and blue. Manda thought it would be fun if the pigeons flew off two days later wearing the Dutch colors red, white and blue. The red became pink and the blue also came out a lot lighter than they had planned.

The girls had started playing badminton, giggling and curious about Didi's reaction. They had had no time to wash themselves in the bathroom. Their hands and nails had a strange grayish tint to them, and particularly Manda's pale legs were covered with red and blue smears.

Didi picked her up with one arm, shook her roughly and whirled her around. At first she squealed, then she started shouting, "Stop, stop, I'm getting sick to my stomach." He didn't pay any attention, not even when she fell silent and turned white as a sheet. Then she started screaming again, "Stop, stop, I'm going to die." Her voice sounded weak and fearful. "Apologize, first," said Didi, who started whirling her the other way just as wildly, her legs high in the air, her tennis skirt all puffed out so that her white sports bloomers with the cut-off legs could be seen. As if this had boosted her injured pride, her voice became strong once more. "Stop, stop," she shrieked, her voice echoing all over the grounds. The servants came out to look, even Cookie came from the kitchen to see what was going on.

"Apologize, first," Didi repeated.

"I'm sorry, I'm sorry."

He set her down on the ground and gave her a playful swat on the behind.

The spark of mischief was already back in her eyes. Her face was still pale, but her lower lip curved down boldly, "The nerve!"

"If you do something like that again I'll shut you up in a cage."

"Just you try it." She granted him her bewitching smile, then took Emma by the arm. "Come on, let's go swimming."

I'm not up to doing anything but waiting here beside the phone, a sheet of white paper and a fountain pen seeking an excuse for why I am the way I am. Justifications, for whom? I wanted to be like Aunt Manda, impetuous, her pure laughing smile an answer to every difficult question, and here I sit and write and write and write, word after word after word, sad about what's disappearing.

Grandma, on your ninetieth birthday, when the orchestra took a break, and newly arrived guests surrounded you, full of admiration for your young radiant appearance, you looked at the beam of sunlight coming in through the parish hall skylight that outshone the dim party lights.

"What are they?" you asked me.

Your trembling fingers attempted to grasp the dust particles in the sunlight.

"Little sunspots, Grandma."

"What pretty words they think of for those little things."

. . .

Didi was still not paying any attention to Manda. Several times a week she went out dancing. She was indefatigable. For her, life consisted of having fun, and she enjoyed dancing, playing tennis, swimming, bicycling, anything that made her body effervesce.

"Will you be my girl?"

"Why?"

"You're the sweetest and prettiest girl I know."

"Oh yeah?"

Emma could hear her mischievous laugh, and peeked outside through the crack in the wooden shutters to see which of the visitors was this time confessing his love to Manda in the alcove in the back gallery. There were those who tried it every day; and there were those who gave up after one try and then chatted up Emma or one of her younger sisters. Emma had seen a lot of boys come and go, and pitied them because they always kept their hopes up that Manda's provocative laugh might have meant "yes."

The war broke out when Manda was fourteen. Didi was called up to leave with the navy. When he came to announce the bad news he was carrying a large black-and-white photograph in which he, dressed in his navy uniform, cap on, looked twenty-eight, not twenty-two. The earnest dark piercing eyes, the little black mustache and the thin determined mouth made him seem older.

"Will you wait for me?"

The fourteen-year-old Manda was speechless and then she laughed.

In saying farewell, Hermanus van Maldegem enveloped his future son-in-law in a firm embrace. With tears in his eyes he said, "She is yours." A moment later he was standing in the hallway of the colonial residence, the entire family around the table, dejected, not only because of Didi's departure, but also because the war had suddenly warmed up the chilly house.

Dressed in his uniform, beads of sweat on his forehead, he entered the family dining room, removed his cap, and saluted Van Maldegem, who got up and spontaneously returned his salute. Out of the inner pocket of his coat Didi magically produced a cockatoo. "Forgive me, Father," he said, because he had been calling my grandfather "Father" for years, bowed toward Manda, who was smiling shyly, and set the cockatoo with a graceful gesture on her shoulder.

The bird wanted to leave the slender shoulder right away and go back to the large hand where it felt at home, but Didi wouldn't allow it. He tickled the animal's neck with his forefinger, at which it muttered, "Hoavyou," like a curse.

"Did you hear that, did you hear that?"

Again the bird uttered, "Hoavyou. . . hoavyou. . . hoavyou."

"What's he saying?" The family's oldest son leapt from his chair and placed his ear close to the cockatoo's beak.

The bird fell silent. It pecked a little at Manda's neck, stepped down from her shoulder onto the table and poked its beak into the platter of spiced *nasi goreng*.

"I love you, he's saying, I love you." Didi was still panting. Proudly he looked from Manda to Hermanus. "It was my father's, and he got it from my grandfather. When my father passed away it became mine. When I first saw Manda, I decided that the cockatoo was going to be her wedding present. I kept it hidden because otherwise it wouldn't be a surprise, but now that the war has intervened she can have the bird if she tells me 'yes' now."

Manda lifted the cockatoo off the table, put it in her lap and stroked it.

"I already said 'yes' a long time ago," she sighed.

She put the bird back on her shoulder and ate a mouthful of rice that had gotten cold.

Didi stood, somewhat embarrassed, in the middle of the room.

"Go on, now," said my grandfather, "go on, my boy, go now, or else you'll be late."

(Not Martin, but all the other men were little sunspots in my hand.)

Aunt Yossa says that sometimes you suddenly say, "Hey, what's that nice young man's name, the one who sometimes grabs me and wrestles with me. A nice fellow. What's his name again?"

"You mean Edwin?"

"Yes, Edwin, now I remember, his name's Edwin. He's a very sweet man, and very funny. I haven't seen him for a long long time."

My father won you over first, when he was after my mother. The war had just ended and, having been a prisoner of war deprived of women for such a long time, he noticed Aunt Manda and my mother walking. They were on their way to school. My mother cheerful, because she learned easily and wanted to become a doctor, and Aunt Manda reluctant, because she hated learning and sitting still, and she actually wanted to marry Didi as soon as possible after he finally got back from Australia where he spent the war years with the navy. They saw him watching them as he, a sergeant-major, shouted "Attention!" and "About face!" to the recruits, with a little extra bass and volume in his voice to make an impression. Aunt Yossa said that he would leave a box with foodstuffs, soap and other luxury items on the doorstep every day. At first you didn't know who the generous donor was, until he let himself be caught after several weeks.

Grandpa never forgave Edwin, I don't think, for avoiding him and his pigeons while winding you and his other daughters around his little finger so quickly. In the pictures from that time I see him in the arms of all your daughters, with two of your daughters in his lap, playing with Manda, or hugging you or Aunt Yossa.

Aunt Manda always tells the same story about my father. He addresses her as "Miss," bows, surprises her every now then by getting her a drink, makes her dizzy when he dances with her, makes her laugh. Her eyes smile when she talks about him and the parties long go in your house.

As a child, I once asked my mother, "Why is Daddy with so many ladies in all the pictures?"

She laughed proudly and said, "Your father is a real charmer."

Could Grandpa have been jealous of Edwin's talent for being able to flirt with any woman without ever being tempted to overstep the bounds of propriety?

My father calls it "self-control." "A man has to know how to control himself," he always said. From my childhood I also remember my mother's friends sitting in his lap. He would run after them if they had sprayed him with the garden hose once again, or they would shove ice cubes down his neck and burst out laughing when he pulled his shirt out of his trousers, cursing, to shake the ice off his back, and sometimes four or five women at once would tickle him until he begged for mercy.

He would toss Aunt Yossa into the air like a football, up toward the ceiling, and wait until she was very close to the ground before catching her.

Did you know that I always thought my father was really in love with Aunt Manda, but that, because she had already been spoken for, he had had to make do with my mother, who was beautiful, sweet and intelligent, but who always wanted to do everything by the book, never made mistakes and always had all the answers.

The story of the cockatoo was told to me many times by Aunt Yossa and by my mother. But I enjoyed listening more to the stories that Aunt Manda would tell me herself when I stayed over in her cramped upstairs apartment. When her boys were in the living room playing with their Matchbox trucks and tin soldiers, she would whisper to me, sitting on the hidden little seat, her sultry voice restrained, a compelling twinkle in her hazel eyes.

"The photograph in the big silver frame I always kept on my dresser. There was this nice boy, very fine to look at, who later became the director of a big company in the States. He always turned the picture around and said, 'He's been dead a long time now. Don't wait for that old guy, he could be your father.' Every day he would come by to ask me if I wouldn't accept his gold ring. I didn't have the cockatoo back yet, because when we went into the camp we gave the cockatoo to Grandma Virginia's oldest daughter, you know, Aunt Fuut, who's now living with Grandpa and Grandma in their house. She was supposed to take care of the bird. Momma had already picked our youngest brother up from the men's camp, and it was at that time that your father was putting all those boxes with rations on our doorstep. 'Don't laugh like that, Manda,' this young man would say. Oh, I can still see his face, looking at me so sadly, and then he lays the picture down again, and then I take the picture and set it upright again. He came by every day, and he cried right before my eyes, he'd get down on his knees in front of me and beg, 'Don't do this to me.' And yet pretty soon after that he was happily married, at least I heard he was happy, from all accounts. Later he would call me from San Francisco once in a while, 'Aren't you sorry, Manda?' 'No, not at all.' Then there was this other boy, his father was Chinese and his mother was half Dutch, half Sumatran. I hadn't expected it of him that he would get all head-over-heels. The cockatoo was back with me again. Aunt Fuut had come to Batavia and brought my bird. I went out with this boy, went dancing, to the movies, the usual, like friends, and the cockatoo always went along. I did that because the bird was a good chaperone. It always sensed if the company I was keeping was trustworthy or not. He thought the bird was beautiful, and would put it on his shoulder or in his lap, or even in his breast pocket if he were wearing a jacket. The bird wasn't shy with him and didn't attack him, so he tried teaching it new words. In the beginning the cockatoo didn't want to talk anymore, he'd just squawk all of a sudden. But later on it did talk, mostly gibberish, as if it were praying. It might well be that it was mumbling something from a prayer, because Aunt Fuut was very devout, just like Grandma Virginia. She prayed quite a few times a day. Still does. Hasn't it ever struck you the way she's still saying grace when we've almost finished supper?

"One day we were at the movies and suddenly the cockatoo mumbled something. I couldn't make out what it had said, but maybe this boy had. He asked me for the first time where I had gotten the bird. I showed him the picture of your Uncle Didi. A little snapshot I always carried in my purse, not that big picture in the big frame, of course. The next day, this boy. . . nobody would have dreamed. He seemed so quiet. I had no idea that he. . . . But sometimes you don't know, there were so many boys. I went out with him in particular because he didn't bother me. He was always well-behaved. Oh well, maybe it had nothing to do with me, maybe he was sick of the war, or maybe he couldn't bear that with the revolution going on there was still no peace. Sometimes you think you know what a person is feeling. But you still don't know anything."

. . .

I dreamed of cockatoos, drew cockatoos in the margins of my math notebook at school, also drew cockatoos when the art teacher instructed us to draw elephants or airplanes. Whenever I was depressed, I would imagine a cockatoo on my shoulder, could feel its beak pecking at my neck and hear it chatter my own poems in my ear.

"After the war it never said 'I love you,' anymore. It said other things, though. You couldn't have that bird around with company because it would talk like a sailor and say things like 'fakmey' and. . ."

"What, Auntie?"

"Fakmey. . . . I'd better not say that again because somebody's going to hear me and then, look out. . . . When his brother left for The Netherlands, Uncle Didi had the bird shipped along since I was laid up in the sanitarium with a hole in my lung. His brother needed money, so he sold the bird over there.

"It was better that way, because later on when we went to Holland we were living in that noisy little house with the paper-thin walls in the Jordaan, that old neighborhood in the center of Amsterdam. Those people are quick to argue as it is and who knows what other sort of dirty talk that cockatoo still knew from the past. Without realizing it you've insulted passers-by and have them to contend with. The cockatoo wasn't used to a cage. That barber below us, you know, our landlord over there, he already made so many comments about the smell of our cooking and things like that, who knows, his criticism might have been a lot worse. And then your uncle was always off somewhere, so I always had to manage by myself."

. . .

He had just left. My lips were still moist from his. My neck was still damp from his tongue, my underwear wet. He had pushed me against the closet and while sucking on my nipples he had fondled me between my legs until I slid, writhing, against his body and down onto the floor. There had been no time for more. Without realizing it, I had managed to undo his belt during our dizzying kisses, and pulled down his fly, let my clasped fingers skillfully grip, rub, stroke, but the antique standing clock in the hall, a wedding present from my in-laws, was unrelenting. In his hurry, he forgot his house keys, which I was able to drop into a drawer just in time before my husband and my parents came in. We all went out into the yard, they sat in the shade and I in the sun, my lips full and swollen with blood from kissing, my laugh hearty, my body languid and hot.

"It's so warm."

"But it's nice."

"Uh-huh, we've been lucky this summer."

"There's going to be a storm later."

I don't want a real conversation. I surrender my face and my limbs to the sun. My skirt is briefly lifted by the breeze.

With my eyes shut I say slowly, "A refreshing wind in the hot sun."

"Had to leave early, then?" asks Martin, my husband, pouring tea and emptying a box of cookies onto a plate.

"The wind?"

"Didn't he want to stay and meet your parents?"

"No, he had an appointment," I lie. My eyes open. I shift in my chair.

"Warm, it's hot," I say.

"Then get out of the sun," says my mother.

"No, I want to feel every moment of summer in my body."

And then she starts telling us a story. She sits up straight,

42

her legs together, her expression serious. There is no introduction, there is no question to which her words are an answer. Martin and I look at each other. My hands tremble. The light is becoming a glare. The heat vexing.

"It was a day like today, muggy, because it was the rainy season. Except that in Indonesia we never sit in the sun, as you know. Siesta time was just getting underway. Everybody had gone to their rooms to sleep, but Manda and I always secretly went bicycling or swimming. Manda liked pulling pranks and I had to go along so she wouldn't be the only guilty one. I think that afternoon we had stolen some mangoes from the parish tree. I'd had to stand guard while she climbed into the tree. The mangoes were still too sour. We waited for Cookie so she could use them to make *rujak* for us. Manda was sprawled in a chair, just like you are now, catching her breath. She hadn't worn anything on her head when she was bicycling and as I recall I was afraid that she might have run up heatstroke or sunstroke. My mother was resting. All of a sudden my youngest sister Eva comes running up. 'Daddy's in love, Daddy's in love,' she shouts.

"'Be quiet,' says Manda, 'you'll wake everybody up.'

"'Daddy's in love with Jacqueline.'

"Jacqueline, like many young people, lived in with us. It was just before the war and she didn't want to live with her parents anymore. A girl of eighteen, nineteen, who worked for my father. She had just started working there as an operator, just like my mother used to, and sometimes she came over to play badminton with us, or bridge, or if there was a party or whatever, because there was always something going on at our house. My father and mother liked having young people around and organized all kinds of things. Grandma was very hospitable and she had been so kind as to take her in. We lived in one of those big colonial mansions with lots of extra rooms

43

along the back gallery. You know what I mean, of course, you've been to Indonesia so many times.

"'Daddy's kissing Jacqueline,' the child shouted again and again as if she were repeating the line of some song.

"'Where?' asked Manda, jumping up from her chair.

"'Daddy crawled into bed with Jacqueline. I saw it through the window.'

"My mother came out of her room because of all the noise we were making, ran to the back gallery, then turned and walked towards us sobbing hysterically in the hallway where she, this is true, I saw it myself, where she beat her head on the marble floor. She had dropped down to her knees. Again and again and again."

She is shaking.

"I can still see her crying. Her forehead is covered with blood. There is blood coming out of her nose. I can see her pulling her hair out of her head, and she keeps saying, 'I want to die, I want to die, I want to die.'"

III

Writing is a way for me to disappear, a way not to wait for him to call, or show up at the door unexpectedly like he used to, with his shining eyes and his cheerful mouth, the nudge in my side, a hand wildly running through my long hair, his beautiful white teeth playfully in my neck, my upper arm, on my earlobe or cheeks. A way not to listen for the mail carrier coming up the path, not to hope that a car is driving up with express mail—because didn't he send everything express, as if there was no time to be lost?—not to flip through my appointment book, trying to decide whom I should call so that I can forget him for a moment?

When I was five, I think five, I saw the world for the first time. Or, actually, the end of the world.

Until then, everything had been us. Everything had smelled familiar, even waiting at the bus stop, my feet like ice, everything around us black, my teeth chattering, my hands under my mother's skirt pressing my nose against her rough winter coat, or in my father's arms breathing in his after-shave and tiger balm. The train, full of unfamiliar faces, smelled just like home because I hid my face under my mother's wide cotton polka dot dress and I was too little to differentiate between the pastures that whizzed by behind the window and the pictures in grown-up books.

In every living room batiks hung on the walls, or there were batiks over chairs or sofas. The rice stuck to my tongue, or the grains would separate and slide from the spoon into my mouth one by one. I could expect little green and red peppers among the vegetables both at home and elsewhere, and the fire in my mouth was just as hot, whether I drank our own fresh-tasting tap water or the water with the funny taste at my grandmother's. Everywhere they laughed when I took a mouthful of white rice to cool off my mouth after the *chabé rawit* sauce and said, "That'll make you big and strong, my girl." If the tears kept flowing there was my father, an uncle, an aunt, Grandma or Grandpa who would pick me up, put me on a chair, turn the music way up, and clap their hands, "Dance, Meisje, dance."

Sometimes we traveled by car, and then I got to see our street, the front of our building, and especially my cousins with whom I was packed into the back seat, waving at the other cars. On sunny days they would put me in the baby carriage with the hood down together with Aunt Manda's second boy, a child who was younger though taller and fatter than I, so that less space was left for me and my head regularly hit the hard rim; then I would be placed on a prickly blanket, surrounded by uncles, aunts, Grandpa, Grandma and the older children. The grass, taller than I as I was sitting there, afraid to move because every movement caused a nasty pricking in my legs, was the fence around our picnic blanket, was the fence around our house as soon as the familiar cake tins, pots, thermoses and enameled tin cups and plates emerged from the baskets.

Before I saw the horizon, I had already walked in the grass, among the tall stalks. I picked weeds myself, harvesting little more than crushed fluff, and tickled everybody's noses the same way they had tried to make me laugh before. They tickled me, threw me into the air; and I would fall asleep beside my plump little cousin, my legs across his stomach and Grandma's sunhat over both our heads to protect us from sun and flies.

One day, after a drive in a full car, we came to a new house. Other people and a strange odor, paint smell I realized later as I kept trying to remember how it was. Aunt Fuut's grandson, Boy, with whom I played hide-and-seek at Grandma's and with whom I had looked in all the dark corners of her apartment, was there too. Lots of light, the strange odor, lots of voices, strangers' legs, strangers' faces, although I couldn't really see any heads, no music, which was odd, only the voices. And then I recognized his socks in new shoes and an unfamiliar pair of pants, his demeanor, his breaking voice, and I rubbed my face on one of his pant legs. My hand gripped his leg, and I smelled him, without having to look up at his face.

He pushed me away, not roughly, but firmly, sat down on the stairs and pulled a girl, bigger and older than I, with long blond hair in braids, black patent leather shoes, more I didn't see, up on his lap. I walked down the hall, tripped over feet, but kept walking to where, as if all by itself, the back door opened at just the right moment. At first still surrounded by legs and voices, then no more noise, I walked all alone to the end of the bare, empty yard, looked over the fence posts still without wire, and saw the end of the world. For a long time I was scared to see that line in the distance, after so much sand with nothing on it.

Later Boy kissed me on my neck like before, pulled me against his crotch until I almost choked but not quite, his songbird seed scent like a warm ribbon through my head, stomach, legs and arms, but it was different after that. The ribbon was cooler, thinner. The fabric of his pants didn't make me hungry anymore.

Grandma, how can it be that your five daughters are so different? The youngest, Eva, who emigrated to Australia, I hardly know. I can still see her dancing. When Grandpa and you weren't at home, she would stand up on the dinner table in her stocking feet and rock 'n roll with your nephews, those dark young men who all played guitar and had formed a band together with the Indies man next door. My other aunt, Divette, who got divorced twice and in both cases married a Dutch man, was less passionate than she was quick-tempered. I often saw her fighting with her husband. If I stayed over with her there was always some china that suffered, or chairs that flew through the room. Her house smelled of beer, never food. I would press my nose against the front windowpane and wait until the woman across the street went out shopping. I imagined she was a witch and thought up magic potions she was concocting in her dark, downstairs apartment where the curtains were always drawn. In my imagination I would turn the husband of this aunt forever crying, even if she didn't get beaten by him, into a cockroach.

Aunt Yossa was a friend, not an aunt. She taught me how to dance, and she taught me to box. "Sticking up for yourself," she called it. I had to practice with my right and my left against the flat of her hand, and at night before going to sleep, when she took off her bra to put on her pink nylon nightie, I had to pound on her back until she had burped and passed enough wind. She would heave a contented sigh, still had me scratch around some or look to see if there wasn't a loose hair on her pale back or shoulder, and say, "Thank you, Meis. Now off to bed."

My Aunt Manda knew about passion, the hot sun hidden in your breath, visible in your eyes' provocative laughter that makes others hungry, greedy, and never satisfied. She taught me to taste the sun. My mother sought a love with moderate temperatures, without wind, no cool breeze by heat, no tearful cheeks by storm with sand that makes the skin tingle. Encouraged by Aunt Manda, a spontaneous laugh might escape my mother now and then, but afterward she would bite her lip, as if she wanted to quell the residual fun.

She brought us up with a fear of frayed fabric and dirty nails, and the pressing worry about whether something in our appearance was peculiar in some way. Due to her unfamiliarity with pleasure, she saw only danger in our pleated skirts whipping up in the wind, our sagging wool knee socks and our fits of laughter, not so much because something might befall us through the appeal in our baring our teeth and legs, but because she dreaded our being offensive and insulting this proper Dutch society. The color of our skin and our hair, she said, was already so noticeable, that gray or beige clothes and modest behavior were necessary to temper our natural difference. As toddlers we were allowed to be attractive: big bright-colored bows in our hair, hand-knit sweaters, dresses with lace and frills, white ankle socks that were set off by our brown legs. But after we were six we were taught to make ourselves as small as possible, not to contradict anyone, only to speak when asked to, always to let somebody have our seat any time, anywhere, to walk without making a sound, never to pass in front of someone unless expressly invited to by the other person, never to laugh with an open mouth, always to look someone in the eye when addressed, and we were explicitly warned that any public show of pleasure, when you looked like us, can be rude.

"Impressing someone," said my mother, "is only justified by outstanding grades at school, by courtesy, by modesty and by well-bred and irreproachable behavior."

You weren't as strict as she was, you didn't make so many demands. I often wondered why she, of all your daughters, had to be so prudish, so strict and dull. When my sister and I would spend the weekend with you, as fourteen-, fifteen-year-olds, and it was Saturday night, you would say, "What are you two hanging around in front of the television for? You're young, you should be going out, dancing, seeing boys, having fun." And then you'd look in *The News* to see if there weren't any concerts, a teen dance or a good movie at the cinema. You'd send us off with too much money and say to us, with a serious look in your eye, "Take a cab home. Spend all of it. Money was meant to flow."

My mother would already be hollering before we'd even left the house, "Be back by ten o'clock." We were sent back to the bathroom to wipe our eyes if there were eye shadow or eyeliner on them. But when we were twelve you took us to the beautician and gave us your leftover nail polish and lipstick.

Even now you touch up your eyebrows with a sure hand and have a soft almost invisible color on your lips that makes your mouth a little fuller, a little more inviting.

My mother doesn't want to depilate her mustache, heavy especially on the right-hand side, it prickles when you kiss her, "because that'll only make it worse." When we were sixteen you gave us a Lady Remington that my mother wouldn't let us use because Aunt Manda had also shaved her legs, in the camp, and as a result still had to do it now. She proudly showed us her legs with the long black hairs on the knees and on the insides of her calves, and said, "Just look, I never did anything, and my legs are still just about smooth."

She forbade us to put on make-up because otherwise we'd

get old too quickly, our skin would get wrinkly and our eyelids would droop.

Grandpa liked it when we dressed up to go out, accentuated our eyes a little and borrowed your high heels. Proudly he let Aunt Yossa take a picture of him with my sister and me, one on either side. He was already shorter than we were, and very thin. "The heart of a young rascal," the doctor had said, "but a stomach like a tea bag." Not long before that he had, after the thousandth operation, received extreme unction from the priest for the third time already; we couldn't possibly have suspected that it would be at least seven years before he would be felled for good by another illness altogether. We had stood around his bed with a lot of other cousins, aunts and uncles, my sister and I as the oldest granddaughters at the foot of the bed. Following the ceremony, during which he had kept his eyes shut, he suddenly scrambled up, blinked his eyes, frowned, and said, "Are you girls going out? Ask Grandma for some money!"

"'Hands up.'

Johan was standing at the foot of my bed with a pistol made of bamboo and rubber bands. He was about seven and I was three. The whole family was staying at Aunt Fuut's in Sukabumi. Grandma Virginia, who was still living with us at the time, had also come along. My little brother Roy was sick, bad diarrhea and cramps. The day before, my mother had shouted for a spoon and then, because it was taking so long, put her own finger down his throat anyway, and he had almost bitten it off. I remember everything. They say that as an adult you can't remember anything from that age, but I can still see Aunt Fuut's yard, and I can still remember that it was quiet and cool in the evenings, because she lived in the mountains.

When we were ready for bed we had to put on little vests over our nightgowns.

"Dinner had been taken home prepared. That's what must have made us sick. Roy almost died. Every time any of us was very sick, my mother had us all drink castor oil. The oil was warmed in a little bowl so it would get thinner and when we'd emptied the bowl we got some candy to get rid of the nasty taste. We all had to go to bed, and only after we'd had three bowel movements were we allowed to get up. Johan was the first to be back on his feet and was playing prisoner's base with your Aunt Yossa, who had snuck out of bed already. She never listened. She'd get spanked by Grandpa, but that didn't bother her. I was the only one lying in bed, because I had a fever. It was one of those big rectangular beds with railings, a mosquito net and copper globes on the four corner posts. I'd grab the big globes when I stood up in bed and I'd lick that cold metal with my tongue. I had two cloth dolls that Grandma Virginia had made for me. I was the doctor and the dolls were sick. Their mouths were embroidered on their faces with red thread that started to pill when I poked it trying to stick my finger into one of the mouths. Because of all the digging around, a little hole got started out of which straw stuck.

"'Hands up.' Johan stood there, legs apart, in his shorts.

"I held my arms up, but I couldn't lift my right arm.

"'Both arms up,' said Johan.

"'I can't,' I said.

"Then he grabbed my arm, lifted it up himself, but as soon as he let my arm go it fell down by itself. He started shouting, 'Mamma, Papa, Grandma, Auntie, Emma's turned into a doll!'

"Because he was screaming bloody murder everybody came running. My mother even left Roy alone for a moment. I was brought to the hospital, and there they lay me in a bed way in back, far from all the other wards, in a separate little room at the end of the garden beside the morgue.

"My father was the only one who was allowed to stay with me. That castor oil was what saved me, the doctor said, a Dutch woman, a very nice doctor whom I saw again later on in the camp. By then she herself had become an invalid from polio. My fault, I used to think. A leg and one of her arms had been paralyzed and had never quite recovered.

"Your Grandpa was with me day and night. He slept in bed with me and told me stories, especially about birds, I recall. I still remember that he mentioned the birds that only make children with each other and go off again. Some birds, I don't remember which ones, lay their eggs in other birds' nests and never look back. Parrots stay together for the rest of their lives, he said, and that's why parrots are tamed so easily, because they become attached to you.

"Visitors weren't allowed to come near me. I'd sit with your Grandpa on a bench in the garden, in the shade of the big palm tree. They were so small, I remember they looked so small, just like dolls, and they waved at me. Closer was forbidden. They just waved. Most times they'd all line up in a row. But Grandma Virginia wouldn't be held back. Your Grandpa said, 'You'll get sick,' and then Grandma Virginia said, 'God has no reason to paralyze me.' She had a present for me rolled up in banana leaves. It was heavy, and I couldn't unwrap it by myself. It was a cast of St. Theresa, and Grandma Virginia said to your Grandpa, 'Pray to her, then she'll get better.'

"You still remember which figurine, don't you? I put it on the windowsill by the little window on the side beside the blessed Mary, with dried flowers and the little bowl of holy water in front. The statuette broke into three pieces in the Japanese camp, and your grandma glued it with egg white. Thanks to the money she earned washing the Japanese soldiers' clothes she was able, in the beginning, to buy eggs at the Chinese shop. In The Netherlands, in the boarding house right after our arrival, while the suitcases were being unpacked, the figurine fell again and broke not only in the same places but others too. For years I kept it held together with tape. Later I could have bought glue, but that was later, and since then the statuette has stayed whole.

"Just before she died, Grandma Virginia gave me a book about St. Theresa, and that's what I took into the Japanese camp. I read about the life of this woman many times. I actually wanted to call you Theresa, because your sister was already named after Grandmother Charlotte, after all, but your father didn't like the idea, he insisted you be called Melanie, after his mother, a prettier name actually, but not used much, you know, because everybody still calls you Meisje. Lucky you're a writer now, so at least strangers will call you by your real name.

"Thanks to blessed Theresa the illness paralyzed only my arm and it has reasonably recovered. Maybe thanks also to the Javanese doctor who massaged me with ice-cold plates with handles on them that I had to press on my arm myself. I can do everything now. Except in the wintertime, because of the cold weather, I usually can't move my little finger, and like yesterday, when I had to go to the bank to get money. . . So I take off my gloves, but I still can't sign because my hand's too cold. Luckily there was an Indies lady, still young, younger than you, a very pleasant woman, who also just says hello to me when I see her in the supermarket or if we meet doing errands by bike. I don't even know her name, but she knows who I am, maybe because of you, maybe she reads your books. She took my hand and said, 'Come on over here, Mrs. Fleurie,' and she started rubbing my hand until it was warm."

• • •

I sometimes think I am married to Martin because he's so like my mother. He is upright, is always ready to stand up for someone else, isn't jealous, knows how to behave himself, respects others, isn't vindictive, has a reason for everything and to my great chagrin sometimes, literally won't hurt a fly.

My mother will always have a plastic fly swatter near at hand in the summer. At moments that you least expect it there will be a resounding smack on the table, on the floor, on the wall. My aversion to flies is not so great that I can stand those unexpected aggressive swats.

"Flies carry illnesses," she'll say. "You have to know how to differentiate between your friends and your enemies." For this reason we had to eat what was on our plates, even when the cake with whipped cream topping was crawling with ants, and we cheered, "Yes!" still unaware of the fauna on the tasty treat when she asked us if we wanted a piece. She had no sympathy for mosquitoes. "There isn't any malaria here, but you can get ugly sores from the bumps," sounded her defense at every deadly blow.

Lotte got the willies from spiders, but if she'd panicked and stepped on a spider to kill it, my mother would teach her to catch the next spider in her hands without hurting its legs and then carefully let it go again outside, no matter how much she hollered and protested.

"Spiders are our friends."

She caught crickets. If we were playing in the square or in the woods across from our house, she would call us to listen to the cricket in her hand. She was insulted at our not wanting to hold the little creature. "Listen how cute," she would say, "that's how they sing, it's beautiful when they all get going together. They do that with their hind legs. Look, you can see, just peek in between my fingers.

"When I was little I would sit out on the porch as dusk was

coming on and listen. My father taught me how to catch them and hold them close to my ear, how to let them sing in my ear and see how they made that sound. When I got infantile paralysis I couldn't do that because I could only use one hand, but then Grandpa would cup my left hand in both his hands and I was able to catch them." She would put the creature in a matchbox. "Here, just listen, it isn't scary this way. Hold the box up to your ear." I quickly did as she said, but promptly thrust the box back into her hand. She kept the box, which was open a tiny crack, finally letting the creature go again after a couple of hours if we continued to ignore it.

She was crazy about dogs. As a child she had had two that she taught to stand on their hind legs and to sit, but here in Holland she didn't want any, no matter how much my father insisted. "It's no life for a dog here," she would say, "you can't do that to an animal, live inside four walls."

Sometimes, very suddenly, my mother could be in high spirits as if the polio hadn't affected her spontaneity. She came back from a vacation trip with you and Aunt Yossa. I was waiting for the bus along with your other grandchildren and Grandpa, and watched how, as the driver lifted Aunt Yossa out of the bus and carefully set her down on the sidewalk, my mother whisked his cap from his head, whereupon he ran after her, and how in a single motion she threw him supply on the grass. All her traveling companions applauded. Grandpa shook his head, but was beaming.

In the days that followed, she would for no reason start horsing around with us at home, tickle Lotte and me until we yelled, "Sorry, sorry," whistle while she cooked, slide over the smooth kitchen floor in my father's gray socks swaying her hips to our favorite music, iron to the rhythm of the radio top ten that echoed all over the house, and stop to chat with everybody while shopping although usually she walked through the stores as inconspicuously as possible. Her playful nudges in my father's side were answered by irritated growls. After some time had passed, everything would go back to the way it was before.

When we were even younger, in the summertime when the days were mild and long enough that the kitchen door could stay open from early morning till late in the evening, she would playfully run after our older cousins, our little brothers or the Indies neighbor boys with a dishtowel that she had rolled from corner to corner and whip it like a catapult at their backsides. Her right arm was weak, but her left arm was all the more developed, and she knew how to work the older boys down onto the floor and would laugh proudly. At moments like that our house was heaven and we were God.

The rest of the time, my mother drudged in silence through her days and couldn't be my role model.

When I wanted to know a lot about us, about before, about who I was and who she was, I asked her to come to Indonesia with me. I wanted to go alone with her to the country of her birth, having traveled there several times with Martin and my son.

At first she complained about everything. The cheap hotels where we stayed were dirty, it was too hot, the rooms were too damp, the beds too soft, the sheets not clean, the people too pushy, the water in the *mandi*-tubs wasn't fresh, everything had changed too much. . . You know how she is.

One of the cities she wanted to see again was Sukabumi. Tired from the ever-so-long bus ride on Java, during which I had become less and less enthusiastic while she had actually gotten more and more excited, we were walking in the tropical rain in search of a tea room. I complained about our not having an umbrella and could see how on both sides of the street the Javanese had taken cover under the wood and corrugated metal awnings. My mother insisted on walking in the rain, because, she said, she had always had a dream of walking in the rain some day like she used to, the climate being warm, not cold and blustery like the Dutch climate.

All of a sudden she took off her sandals, tucked them into the pockets of her divided skirt and began to skip, singing a song in Malay that I had never heard on her lips before. She jumped into puddles on purpose and splashed around with her bare feet in the black mud. The churned-up black water spattered up on her legs. Her beige skirt got splotched, but she laughed aloud. More of a laugh than Aunt Manda's, more of a laugh than a laugh can laugh.

"Are there a lot of those books?"

That was the first thing I said to him.

In the display case lay an open bibliophilic edition, carefully crafted for friends and collectors, of a poet unknown to me and illustrated by an artist likewise unknown to me. The lithograph on the left page, hard yellow and the color of meat, brown and red with delicate, tentative black lines, and the hand-set text to the right made my annoyance at the long drive, my disappointment over the newest paintings done by my friend Brose, a fifty-year-old artist to whose shows I had too often promised to go without actually making the effort, disappear. Martin had been buttonholed by a gallery owner. He was a striking figure in his white shirt, crinkled indigo linen jacket, his combed-back hair and his unforgettable face. I do notice them—as he gets older and the lines in his face only make him more fascinating and his graying temples make his tanned skin shine and light up his pale gray eyes—those women of all ages who look at him, accidentally bump into him or ask him what time it is. But I am proud of him, not jealous like I used to be over twenty years ago when we were first together.

Martin motioned to me. He hates receptions, but once there he manages better than I do. He'll talk to strangers, seems to be constantly entertaining himself, but is always prepared to go home at a moment's notice. I wasn't in the mood to mingle. In those days I didn't want to see anybody, wrote poems, no stories, no novel. There was a manuscript of mine that I had once let a publisher read. He had responded enthusiastically, but so totally in the wrong way, that I'd taken the work back to let it rest for a while. I wanted to stay in bed that Saturday, but Martin had prodded me to get up, saying that it would be unfair to Brose to blow him off again.

Having strayed away from the people and from the bright carnavalesque paintings, my eye fell on the display case. There were many collector's editions, but particularly this one, bound in brown leather like the scaly skin of a *salak* fruit, spoke to me.

The body of a small dead bird, no, the bird was alive and yet it radiated something of death, there was a brief association with the smell that drifts out of the always open door of the poultry shop in our new pedestrian mall; it communicated pain despite the smile that the crested bird wore at the corners of its beak. The text, fragile because of the way in which the classic lettering was printed on the paper, made me forget the smoke, the constant murmur of the public and the visitors' overbearing perfume.

"You pulled my feathers out / I didn't scream / I gave my smile / willingly / the colors of my crest / have remained upright / and yet I tremble / when your nails hotly / forget that I've been plucked."

A man came and stood across from me. I watched the way he leaned on the glass of the case with both hands, their backs covered with hair, slender fingers, clear nails cut neither too short nor too long. His fingers were shaking.

When I looked up at his face past his hands, his timeless

navy blue suit, nondescript tie and white shirt that bulged at the waist, I saw a round head covered with similarly thick hair, small round glasses in front of green-brown eyes. I took him for a co-owner of the gallery by the hungry way he was looking at me.

"I'm responsible for all the books in this case," he said, "that book, too," and he pointed at a smaller book that lay open, in which I recognized Brose's work.

"Would you have another one?" I clarified my meaning by pointing at the plucked bird, more naked than people without clothes on.

"Oh, excuse me, of course, it's an edition of fifty, and the book only just came out, but I'll go ask one of the gallery owners if there are any more in stock here. If not, I can personally offer you this one, if you like. How many were you thinking of?"

"I just want one, that is, only if I can afford it," I said.

He laughed. "We shouldn't discourage young people with an interest in art. Do you have a moment? Walk to my car with me. I'll make you a gift of a copy for the symbolic amount of a hundred guilders."

"That's impossible, it's kind of you, but I'm sure the book is worth a lot more."

"If you don't want the book for a hundred guilders, then I'll give you the book as a gift. But how did you become interested? Do you know the painter, the poet?"

"I don't know either of them, but it's as if I once wrote the text myself, and I like the bird, the bird is beautiful."

"Yes, the plucked cockatoo is one of the most beautiful themes in his work."

"Cockatoo, of course, a cockatoo."

"Do you like birds?"

"The cockatoo is very special to me. I used to dream of

someone giving me a cockatoo as a present."

"Not anymore?"

"Actually, I'd forgotten about that dream."

I got to know Martin in high school. He was a senior and I was a sophomore when we first met. I thought he was arrogant because he put my cabaret lyrics down as too childish, and he claimed three years later that he had been head-over-heels in love and had wanted to impress me. I dropped out of the cabaret group and avoided him. If I saw him riding into the school yard on his moped, I would quickly walk into the building. In the halls I'd dodge into an alcove or the toilets if I saw him approaching in the distance. He soon finished his exams and disappeared out of my life for several years. I saw him again only when I myself was about to take my finals and he and I ran into each other at the school reunion. He apologized and said, "I was pretty macho back then."

He won my father over without even noticing. The first evening he came to see us there was a soccer match on television. After a quick handshake from my mother, a kiss from my littlest brother and a nod from my other little brother, already nestled up on the couch beside my father, Martin sat down on the other side. I stayed in the room for a bit, then went upstairs to do my homework. "By-y-e," he called up, in a hurry to catch the last train to the university town where he lived. After that he came by every Sunday evening on the way back to his place after spending the weekend at his parents' house. He came to watch sports in our living room because, like him, my father and my brothers were Ajax fans, whereas his father, to his embarrassment, cheered when Feyenoord was doing well.

In only a few months Martin and my father were teaming together against the rest of the world. It was Martin who became aware quite quickly that Grandpa didn't see eye to eye with my father. Because I promptly denied it, he asked me to watch how they behaved toward one another. I noticed they weren't friends like Grandpa and Didi, but that they tolerated each other. Like birds they marked off their turf with the sounds of their voices and neither let the other in.

Martin, however, was chummy with Grandpa. When you still had no idea that Grandpa even had cancer, Martin already knew how it had metastasized, and one time Grandpa took him along to the specialist. Martin, who's been living with me for twenty-two years now, quickly became one of the family. If Martin once again unthinkingly went to sit in your sacred spot on the couch and all of us shouted in chorus, "That's where Grandma sits," you would say, "Let him be, Martin can sit there."

And yet, when Martin came over to me with a spring roll on your ninetieth birthday, you asked me, "So, who's that man?"

"That's Martin, Grandma."

"Martin?"

"Yes Martin, my husband."

"Oh, are you married now?"

"I have been for a long time, Grandma, for a very long time, remember?"

"Oh, I forgot all about it. But he's so old! I just don't recognize him anymore. You're so young and that's such an old man. Oh well, as long as you're happy, right?"

I hadn't paid much attention to the word. But I had heard the word "swimming" mentioned once or twice.

On the boulevard, the wind and in the distance, blue, the endless sky above the other blue, water that isn't sleeping, almost comes close in a white rage, but doesn't. The grains of sand between our toes, although I wouldn't hear of taking off my shoes and socks. My summer dress and even my warm cotton cardigan with wooden buttons I kept on as I leaned against the wall. Above me, the boulevard. (A beautiful word, boulevard, I thought; bulbul birds and sailing far. I never thought it would be a street with buildings on one side and the horizon on the other.)

Two of my cousins, a boy and a girl with only her under-pants on, ran back from the sea towards us to where our tow-els lay folded on the tote bags with buns and thermoses. The sand flew up and settled on my ankles and calves, in the hol-low behind my knee and I quickly wiped the grains from my legs. Where the sand stuck I slapped it off with demonstrative pats.

The boy took a big towel.

"That's big," said Lotte.

"Bath sheet," said the boy shaking out the towel, sand in my eyes; the sand on my lips tasted salty. He laid it on the ground, pulled the corners straight, right on the loose sand, that clean towel, and lay down on it, his eyes closed, heaving a sigh.

Goose bumps on his stomach around his navel. Drops of salt water on his chest. An opening in his wet briefs, an open-ing, dark, no color, just little curls. I squinted to look under his briefs at his hidden skin. Nol, the Dutch boy, thirteen, fourteen years old, choir and altar boy—I wanted to go to mass when his name was printed in the parish paper—was sitting on my little brother's tricycle, whereby the wide leg of his shorts exposed the same curly hair and something else, which I had never seen, that dangled, different from my brothers, different because he was Nol, not a little brother, not a father, not an uncle, but Nol, who never took any notice of me, though he did fool around with the girl next door the same age as I was:

big black eyes, long lashes, shorter, prettier, nicer, with long ringlets made with an electric curling iron.

Looking at Nol was the ribbon in my stomach and head and hands, just as with my boy cousins behind the door or behind the curtain to my grandmother's foldaway bed. But now with a little bit of tearing in my chest, a nasty pain that ached together with the hot ribbon that flowed and that I could still remember in bed, although without the tearing feeling because I briefly imagined the girl next door dead, not really dead, but far away, maybe sleeping never to wake up, just gone, gone far away. I stood I don't know for how many hours and looked at the darkness of his skin under his wet briefs drying in the sun and the wind while the sand whipped into my face. This was the first time I had tasted the sea, ever so carefully, the sea which I had imagined would be like our blue swimming pool with grass and tiled floors, trees and a tall fence all around, a towel on the grass or on the stones. The sea is his briefs and the ribbon, from looking and looking and looking while he is sleeping, or in any case has his eyes shut, unaware that I can see him breathing.

"How was the sea?" my mother asks.

"I didn't go in."

Lotte complains about the dirty sand that gets everywhere, about the salt on her lips, the sea that moves, that doesn't lie still like the swimming pool which she misses. My mother laughs. I can see the pride in her face; we, just like her, don't like sand under our nails, wind in our hair or the sultry transpiration of the sea.

IV

Do you believe in coincidence?

Martin and I were sitting at the kitchen table talking. We had gotten up late that Monday morning. He had been reading a book until about two the night before and I'd been up even later writing in my workroom. As a response to the cockatoo in the bibliophilic edition, for which I hadn't been allowed to pay a thing, I had started writing down childhood memories. I remembered a dream I'd had as an eight-year-old and that I'd noted down very awkwardly in my first diary. There was little writing on that page. The greater part of the page was filled by two cockatoos I had drawn and colored in. The cockatoos in my dream had been pink and this is the way it is recorded in my diary: "I dreamed about pink cockatoos. I asked Momma if there are such things and she says there are. But Aunt Manda got a white one from Uncle Didi long ago. Lotte says it is stupid to dream about pink cockatoos and that I am lying because you cannot dream in color, but I saw the colors myself. I will not write down what the cockatoos did because that was very bad. I did not tell anybody."

Martin read the seven pages I had written that night on my word processor. I studied his face as he was reading.

"That dream you had at eight was very special. Two pink cockatoos, one on either side of you, pecking at your bare buttocks with their hard beaks. I wish I had had dreams like that as a child. But the thing that really strikes me is that last night of all times you copy that dream from your thirty-year-old diary and on the basis of this you start writing, while at the same time I'm in our conjugal bed reading an anthropological book, thinking: I'll have to tell Meisje about this. If I hadn't been asleep by the time you came up, I certainly would have, but then we would probably have lain around talking all night."

"What do you mean?" Actually, I was disappointed because he had started in about some anthropology book while I'd given him seven pages of intimate memories. And when Martin eagerly got up from the breakfast table to get Malinowski's book from his desk so he could read me the section, I snatched the sheets of paper from the kitchen table, insulted, to put them away in my workroom. Martin followed me. I was moodily leaning against the wall while he stood on the threshold and read me this folktale from the Trobriand Islands, east of Papua New Guinea:

"*The White Cockatoo and the Clitoris.* A woman named Karawata gave birth to a white cockatoo, who flew away into the bush. One day Karawata went to work in the garden, telling her *kasesa* (clitoris) to look after the *kumkumuri* ([big flat mound-like] earth baking oven). The *kasesa* replies confidently: *Kekekeke.* But the white cockatoo has seen everything from the bush; he swoops down and strikes the clitoris, who cries out plaintively: *Kikikiki,* and topples over, while the cockatoo eats the contents of the oven. . . .

"Next day, Karawata says again to her *kasesa*: "Let us catch pig, get some yams, and bake it all in the earth." Again she takes off her *kasesa*, and leaves it to look after the oven, and the *kasesa* says confidently as before: *Kekekeke*. Again the white cockatoo descends from the branch, strikes the *kasesa*, who, with a plaintive *kikikiki*, topples over; and again the cockatoo eats the contents of the oven. Next day the woman says: "I shall go to the garden and you look properly after the food." *Kekekeke* answers the *kasesa*, but all that happened on the two previous days is repeated, and Karawata and her *kasesa* die of hunger."

Martin had only just finished the last word when the doorbell rang. I sat down at my desk, turned on the computer, and said, "Will you get the door?"

"Meis, it's for you."

Reluctantly I left my workroom. From the kitchen I could see a man holding a big white cockatoo in his hands. The creature was screeching and the yellow crest on its head was erect like a fan.

"Did you order a cockatoo?" Martin asked.

"Of course not."

"Are you Melanie Fleurie?" inquired the man.

I nodded, looking questioningly at Martin who shook his head, "I know nothing about this."

"Then this cockatoo is for you, ma'am, that's what's on the order, deliver to Melanie Fleurie. Could you take it? I have to go get something else out of the van."

There I was, shaking, with a big white cockatoo that stood eighteen inches tall, I, who had never wanted animals in the house because we did so much traveling. Certainly no birds that you have to keep caged up.

The man returned with an antique copper cage big enough to hold me, with a large opening for a door, but no door.

"Would you sign here, ma'am?"

He held a form under my nose while I was trying to keep the big parrot that had stepped from my hand onto my shoulders to investigate my hair and my neck with its beak, under control.

"I didn't order a cockatoo," I said.

Martin stepped forward, "Who placed the order?"

"I didn't get a name, the generous party wanted to stay anonymous. All I know is that I'm supposed to deliver it here. It's a very special parrot, ma'am, the tamest in the world, I was told, and they made sure I understood that I was supposed to handle it with care because it was a pricey little shipment. The shipping costs were all prepaid, so you don't owe me anything."

"Great, imagine that," said Martin. "That's the least they could do."

He looked the man's paper over for an address or a name or a city, any clue concerning the donor.

The creature uttered unintelligible squawks. It flapped its wings when Martin came too close to it.

"Can I also refuse to accept it?" I asked.

"Of course not," said Martin, his mind made up, "we're not going to do that, that isn't nice. But isn't there any explanation or a letter?"

"There is a sheet on the bird's care that I was supposed to deliver along with it," said the man. He pulled out a rolled-up parchment with a red ribbon around it, a frivolous bow and a seal with a thumbprint in it.

The man spurred himself into action. "Have fun with the little feller, ma'am," and he pulled the front door shut behind himself.

"I know who sent it," said Martin, "the man with that book, that's got to be it."

"But why? Why?"

"You'll have to ask him. . . he's in love, of course, head-over-heels in love, I knew that already when I heard that he'd given you that expensive book. He wants to make an impression, like so many men do. But to be honest, your suitors' gifts up till now were never this original. The man does have a certain charm."

And for Martin that was the end of the matter. He still had a smirk on his face, standing there with Malinowski's book *The Sexual Life of Savages in North-Western Melanesia.* He glanced down again at the big cage that took up most of the hallway, back at the cockatoo that was restlessly moving back and forth on my shoulder and grinned again.

"Aren't you scared of cockatoos?"

"I don't know yet," I replied.

Martin tried to take the creature from me as I broke the seal and unrolled the parchment, but the cockatoo was determined to keep stepping back onto my shoulder. I tacked the parchment to the closet door. Together we read the calligraphy of the instructions. At the top it said, "Choose your own name for this cockatoo, for that is how you will create your own bond with this unique bird who may already be a hundred years old and have survived many caretakers. Circumstances have unfortunately required this cockatoo to leave its former owner, but there is no better owner than you, queen of the wingèd word."

Below followed instructions for the bird's feeding, a description of the dangers that could confront it indoors and of its hygiene.

"Call it Kasesa," said Martin.

. . .

I didn't know I had a clitoris. It was only after I'd been going out with Martin for half a year, after we had tried all kinds of ways to make love and I still hadn't had an orgasm, that I started reading books in which the clitoris was written about and tried to find it between my vaginal lips with a little mirror. When I accidentally touched the little bump with my fingernail, moments, dreams, fantasies that had caused the same tingling in my body shot through me. The ribbon, that ribbon that was always there when Martin felt my breasts with his hands, took my nipples between his fingers, let his lips glide from my neck by way of my back, underarm, stomach to my vaginal lips, was different than those jolts that made my body jerk, as if I had no control. But neither Martin, nor the young men before him, had ever discovered my clitoris, or had always avoided it because they couldn't imagine that we girls had something in our vaginas that might be important for their climax. I almost don't dare to ask, Grandma, but I really want to know, because it's something that after a lot of hesitation I also questioned my mother about without getting a clear answer: did you, or do you, know that you have a clitoris? Did Grandpa know? Did you have orgasms?

Because Martin thought it was important that I should have not only the blind, lusty heat that I called the ribbon, but orgasms just like he did, I went, nineteen, twenty years old, the same age my son is now, and asked my girl friends if they knew the high that made men relax so and get so sleepy, that seemed to give them renewed energy, while I, still intoxicated by the ribbon, never called it quits, remained excited, hid my nose in his armpit when, after hours of making love, he fell asleep anyway, and in my imagination let his hands and his tongue slide over my limbs for the hundredth time.

Looking back, I remember twitches I could call orgasms

because they swept me up to heights where I forgot everything, where color, smell, cold and heat became one, where thoughts emptied, twitches never caused by stimulation of that puny little knob between my vaginal lips, but, as I thought then, sometimes by love, sometimes by curiosity, sometimes by the surprise, sometimes by taboos or incomprehensible dreams, sometimes by a body heavy and warm on mine, absolutely quiet, not a word, not a sigh, no Meisje looking at Melanie or the other way around.

My only son is still a toddler and Lotte has had her first child, a daughter, who is staying at my mother's. I'm standing beside my mother as she puts a clean diaper on the baby, I've forgotten how to do all that already; and it's so different with a girl.

"You both have time now to start on a second one."

"I don't even want to think about it."

I follow my mother's hands. She uses her right arm as much as her left, even though she doesn't have any force in it and it's a lot slower than the left one.

"Undo that pin, will you? My right hand doesn't want to cooperate."

It's as if she changed my son with more tenderness and care. Or had I just seen it differently? She would play with him a long time, blow on his stomach until he crowed with delight. She had been the first one to get him to laugh. Three days a week she took care of him as if he were her own child.

She walks into the kitchen to get a wet washcloth while I keep an eye on the baby. The child is looking around contentedly, smiles at me, she is early to smile, not like my son who seldom cried but likewise seldom yielded up his laughter, and one by one sticks her feet in her mouth, lets her legs flop back down, and then with one hand searches around between her legs, where the little fist stops and the little fingers dig, then firmly grasp her vulva, the expression in her eyes hazy. Fascinated by her face which betrays pleasure, I observe the child in silence, wondering whether I ever did that, because I don't remember anything, nothing at all.

"Boo!"

Not only the baby, but I too, am startled. My mother laughs, and right away she wipes the tepid wet washcloth first over the baby's face and head, and then almost roughly cleaning the vulva and the crack in its bottom. When the baby pouts, she quickly picks it up from the table and presses it to her chest, humming hastily, to avoid a crying fit.

The child splutters.

I, too, feel caught red-handed.

With the anger still partially between my teeth, I ask, "Why did you do that?"

"I always did that, I did that with you, too."

"Why?"

She knows I'm accusing her. Her eyes exhibit honest amazement.

Again I ask, because she is silent, "Why did you do that?"

"I learned that from my mother."

"From Grandma?"

"Yes, she always did that, too."

"And where did she get the idea, then?"

"I don't know. Maybe from her mother. . . or from Grandma Virginia. . . . That was just the way it was done. You simply have to teach a child that it can't touch down there. . . ."

"You do?"

"A little one like that will be fiddling with itself the livelong day otherwise."

"Then you scared me enough, because I was almost twenty

when I had to read it in a book that it's a nice feeling to rub my hand in between my legs. Do you actually know that it feels good?"

I can hear my voice, hard and full of reproach.

She has put the baby back down on the table, is powdering its crotch. She mumbles, "You all live in a better time that you can know all those sorts of things."

It's true, my hands had lost their way to my crotch, but something in me had remembered that tingling sensation and sought it in different ways, in the transition from hot to cold; and what would otherwise perhaps have been reserved for my crotch now spread out into every millimeter of my skin. At that time I called it a ticklish warmth, the hot ribbon that roamed through my body. There was no pattern, just the surprise, the unexpected, that dulled my thinking and changed waiting into now. Sitting in Werner's lap, one of my uncles who was too young to be called uncle, but too old to be just another cousin, while he played guitar, sitting there on his thigh feeling his body around me like a coat, I would sink into an intoxicated state that I would, in retrospect, call "voluptuous," but because almost the only thing I can remember from my earliest childhood are those moods and because I can't imagine that as a toddler, a tot, a child, I would always have had the same aim in mind, I think the appropriate word for those moments has to be "sensual." The guitar he held in both hands pressed against my stomach, a prison of music, his warm song against the back of my head. The rhythm of the leg I was sitting on.

. . .

Grandma, did you have the kind of dreams you knew it was best not to tell anybody about? Or were you really innocent, just like Aunt Manda who sees only benign motives behind a man's charming gestures and who never feels called upon to answer for what she has brought about with her seductive smile.

I also knew that innocence, a fenced-in longing, or should I say a caged-up happiness, no, intoxication like this knows no bars; it was the familiar walls of our house, our nest, where, it's true, fiddling with your crotch was punished by a loud "boo," but where communal excitement was encouraged while nobody warned us of the wide expanses that would one day seek to restrain our unbridled sensuality in other ways.

While I was at college I was confronted by men who, as they put it, were calling me to account for my unconscious behavior. To start dancing spontaneously because I happen to run into a group of musicians on the street playing jazz with heart and soul despite the drizzle, to forget myself, get caught up in the movements, and be only laughter. . . . That was happiness, when I was young and still didn't know that some of the men at whom I smiled in all innocence experienced my behavior as inviting and would let me know about it. Either I had to have sex with them or I shouldn't smile at them anymore. There was no compromising. My professor of sexology taught us that naiveté in the sexual arena was merely an attempt to avoid responsibility. Each gesture, each action in relation to someone else, was meant to arouse desire, he said, was a sexual act, and all you had to do was to become conscious of this fact. There is no such thing as innocence.

During that period of my life I became nostalgic for days gone by, when we were allowed to get out of bed in the middle of the night to take part in the dancing going on in the living room. We in our pajamas, you all in your finest clothes. Some

74

of my uncles would roll up their shirt sleeves because of the heat, and some of my aunts would kick off their pumps; my father danced in his socks, my mother always had those plaid slippers on. Maybe it was because I was light and slight of build that they called me Meisje, "Girl," and would pop me on the table or on a chair and cry, "Dance, Meisje, dance." Grandpa taught me the fox-trot and the Viennese waltz when I was just starting to read. You and my aunts taught me all the other steps. I was four when I sang "Send Me the Pillow" with Aunt Manda's second son, stepping out little squares among the other dancing couples to the rhythm of the music.

The beds in which we had slept earlier that evening were to be occupied by our parents, and mattresses were unrolled for us in the living room on which, while the aunts unfolded the clean sheets and put pillowcases around the sofa cushions, we horsed around with Grandpa, Aunt Yossa and one another until we collapsed gasping for breath. The tired ones had already found a mattress corner and were asleep. I reserved a spot next to Aunt Manda's second son who was warm when he slept and who threw his legs around me like a blanket.

During that period of my life I was writing a book about the past. Nostalgia for my innocence.

Aunt Manda said, "Not every man knows his limits."

Grandma, happiness to me is surrendering to sensation, experiencing nothing but pleasant stimulation of my senses, preferably all of them at once, or of one so the others go to sleep. The ribbon, in other words. . . . That's why writing, if I'm successful at submerging myself in my imagination to such an extent that the word becomes the truth, is just as satisfying as the ribbon.

· · ·

Yesterday none of my male cousins came to my party. Aunt Manda was there, came all by herself on the bus, with three transfers, as cheerful as always. She could tell by my face that I had been crying all morning and said, "Does turning forty bother you?"

"No, it's something else."

"Are you in love?"

"No, I was."

"But if it's over, then there isn't anything to feel guilty about anymore, is there? Being in love means you're alive, that you haven't fallen asleep yet." Her eyes sparkled as she spoke. The familiar bold smile played around her provocative lips. "Your heart wasn't captured just because you got married. The point is how you behave. As long as that is pure."

That evening I kept being asked who that charming lady might be. They estimated her age not to be over fifty, but she's already sixty-five, and at her birthday party, to which I went, but you didn't because you were staying with your youngest daughter in Australia, she was walking around with a hand-made button on her cotton suit that said, "Glad To Be A Senior."

In the beginning, Kasesa was afraid of company, but yesterday, even though the bird had never seen her before, it climbed without hesitation from my shoulder to hers when she arrived, and stayed there while she danced. She said it had spoken to her, but that because of the loud music—friends of mine had brought their instruments and were jamming—she wasn't sure if she had understood right.

I looked for and found his first letter and reread it a few times. Every three days, sometimes more often, he had sent letters. Then when we became lovers, he didn't write anymore

76

really, except now and then he'd send a postcard he'd bought at some museum while he was on vacation with his wife. Now I'm surprised if he gives me a quick call from a phone booth when I've been waiting for days, sometimes even a week, for news.

Moss is already growing over our hearts.

Dear Melanie,

After a week's stay in the drizzly Netherlands, surrounded by art dealers and busybodies, almost all of whom have but one ambition: to please, flatter and rip off the bourgeois public (*with* money), it was a true revelation for me to meet someone who knows how to look through the bird's feathers, someone brimming with enthusiasm, beauty and presence.

At that moment I had no idea that this fleeting encounter over a display case at some gallery would haunt me for days.

What, for heaven's sake, did this, as I learned later, celebrated writer think of this exalted Fleming? (My father is Flemish, but my mother is of French-Spanish origin with, in addition, an Algerian grandmother, so like you I am of mixed blood!) A businessman wearing a tailored suit for the occasion, who had the nerve, when she voiced her admiration with few but well-chosen words for the poet and the artist who did the book *The Dilemma*, to say to her, "We should encourage younger people who are interested in art." (Please accept my mistake as a compliment, when I confess to you that I took you for a student at the Art Academy. . .)

I turned red when I heard Brose say that he admired you for your work, and, still under the illusion that he was perhaps teaching you at the academy, I asked which direction you had chosen, consequently hearing from an insulted Brose what a list of titles you had already published. May I put forward as mitigating circumstances that my chronic absence from the Dutch language and literature as well as my limited free time (feeble excuse), and most likely my unjustifiable disinterestedness in contemporary prose have compounded to prevent my recognizing you.

(In the meantime, by the way, I hauled all your titles from the bookstore in a trunk, and am taking two weeks off to read your work.)

Out of sheer clumsiness, after our short walk in the drizzle to my car where I stammered something and placed *The Dilemma* in your hands, I again approached you with the question as to whether you were interested in meeting the artist or the poet who had done the book. . . as if I were doing you a favor. Thanks to your friendly "Yes, please," I could permit myself to ask you for your address and hope to see you again soon. (Sorry, I couldn't think of anything better at that moment.)

I hope you and the cockatoo are managing to get along. Has he said anything yet? That the choice fell on him has nothing to do with the fact that he is probably the tamest cockatoo in Europe, or that his noble white feathers and his large yellow crest demand respect, but because he (among others!) says the words that I myself don't dare to say to you, but which are burning on my lips.

Until soon, I hope,
Neo Pecoque

P.S. I was hesitant for a long time to send you this note. A less fortunate predecessor was ordered to leave you alone for as long as you lived, I was just reading in *Dance, Girl, Dance*, the novel with which you made your debut.

Enclosed: The bird's tags, a kind of ID, so you can take it

across borders, and a few accessories for in the cage. The cockatoo is used to living in an open cage. If you would like a door put on anyway, I can recommend someone who can fit in a grill on hinges with a little latch, at my expense, of course. I have assumed, however, that I might conclude solely on the basis of your smile, your body language, the look in your eye and perhaps, in the meantime, also your books, that you would never wish such imprisonment on anyone.

"A woman must always be strong," you said. "A woman really must always be strong."

In your eyes was a gaze that would lead one to surmise. "A people cannot be cruel. War is cruel and war releases the cruel side of humans." Words from your mouth that preferred to remain silent. "Because we didn't decide for ourselves that we had to be enemies. Others decide who our enemies are and who our friends are, not us. . . . You're supposed to hate each other, but in fact maybe you like each other."

Almost immediately on being interred by the Japanese, Manda, along with a dozen white girls between fourteen and twenty, were designated by the head of the camp and then taken to the building where the Japanese soldiers would drink at night and sing songs. Charlotte let seventeen-year-old Yossa take care of her younger sisters, taking her youngest son, then only eleven, by the hand in order to escort her second daughter, who was ordered by the guards to get into line with the rest of the girls, to the hall. Holding her other hand was the trembling Manda, who didn't understand what was expected of her and the other girls. Once in the dark building, however, she watched a seventeen-year-old auburn-haired Indies girl, together with whom she had repaired the straw roof on one of the barracks only yesterday, with fascination. The redhead let herself be pulled onto some Japanese officer's lap, allowed herself to be held and thirstily drank the glass he offered her.

Charlotte refused each drink that was offered either herself or Manda. She sat straight as a board on a wooden stool and stared straight ahead, Manda's head buried under her arm.

The camp's commander barked at some Japanese subordinates to throw both her and the boy out, but Charlotte acted as if she were deaf and dumb. The boy sat in her lap and she held her arm tightly around Manda's shoulder. With a stoical look on her face she ignored everything that went on around her. A tall broad-shouldered Japanese with remarkably large almond-shaped eyes and opaline skin made a reassuring gesture to the camp commander, offered Charlotte a mug of tea and said in perfect Malay, "Come with me, madam. I won't harm either you or your daughter." Charlotte left the tea untouched and didn't look at this man with his friendly smile either. Then the officer pulled up a wooden bench, sat down facing her, set the tea down beside himself on the bench and pulled out a cardboard wallet. Charlotte peered keenly from under her eyelids, watched as his long slender fingers opened the wallet and took out a photo of a Japanese woman with a girl Manda's age, as he laid his right hand on his chest, over his heart, and lowered his eyes. After this silent gesture, he offered her the tea again. Then he said, "Please come."

By way of many narrow passages, dark spaces, dank damp storage places where they had to step over crates, they reached an open field from which they were able to walk back to the barracks where Yossa and her sisters were waiting. The officer's jaw dropped in amazement when he saw the table-high Yossa, a cigarette clamped between her long fingers, hopping nervously from one short leg to the other. Yossa, crippled by a stiff right leg, sobbing as a result of the tension accumulated over the hours, ran toward Manda, her right leg swinging through the air at every step, and delightedly lifted up her younger sister who was twice as tall and obviously twice as heavy as she was. Tears of joy rolled down her adult face and dripped onto her mature bosom while she tightly hugged Manda, whose waist she reached. But Manda still had no idea from what she had escaped.

The officer patted at his clothing, felt his pockets and magically produced a cigarette which he offered Yossa. A beaming smile appeared on Yossa's face. She bowed deeply a few times, her right leg far out to the side to maintain her balance, her large head almost reaching her ankles, which was a comical sight. But the officer didn't laugh.

In turn the man bowed deeply to her and Charlotte, opened his hands, the pale inviting palms towards the gorgeous mother, barely forty, with the looks of someone of twenty-six, at most thirty, and her remarkable children, as if he were encouraging them to come into his arms. Then he placed both hands on his heart. Charlotte fled, roughly pushing the children ahead, into the barracks, not out of fear of the friendly Japanese, but out of fear of the ribbon that was flowing through her body.

During the evening of the next day when everybody was already asleep, except for Charlotte who was sitting in the moonlight trying to patch the girls' worn dresses with some bits of cloth she had cut from one of Hermanus's forgotten ties, he brought some Javanese cane sugar wrapped in a banana leaf and a few cigarettes for Yossa, "*yang kechil,*" the little one. He remained modestly at a distance. Charlotte did not invite him to sit down beside her on the *tikar.* They said nothing, looked at one another until he lowered his eyes and Charlotte rolled up the *tikar* as a sign that it was time for him to leave.

More than an ear and a smile you didn't offer, but he, grateful for that little bit, rewarded you with a job as washerwoman and in secret brought sugar or rice to feed the eager mouths of your children. Some of the starch you received to iron the uniforms you put aside to make a gruel so that particularly Manda, who was growing, wouldn't complain of hunger. Maybe you wanted him, too, and fought against the temptation to lay your head in his lap, the ball of his thumb in your mouth, his hand in your hair, his lips whispering down your willing ear toward your mouth, your neck, your proud breasts and the weak hollows of your body.

What's wrong with love?

Could this be an appeal to justify my own behavior, which is actually far less answerable than any possible relationship between you and that sympathetic officer, The Enemy?

Did you feel that desire but want to be brave, strong, faithful to your husband, faithful to a flag, faithful to the queen of a country where you had never been, or faithful to yourself?

Where did you get the strength not to feel?

Martin, too, knows that I tried to keep that French-Spanish Fleming out of my life.

Dear Mr. Pecoque,

My husband and I were terribly surprised when a courier from Belgium dropped off a beautiful white cockatoo with a blindingly yellow crest.

I don't know to what we owe this lively gift, but after some initial trepidation, I now dare to promise you that my husband and I will do our very best to take good care of Kasesa (that is what we christened the bird).

Can it really talk? We have been unable to make sense of any of the diverse calls it has let us hear since it came to our modest home, but perhaps it speaks Arabic, Chinese or Finnish, or some other language we can't recognize or don't know.

Once again, my thanks for this colorful, exotic gift we still don't really know what to do with.

Yours truly,
Melanie Fleurie

P.S. Don't worry, the cage will remain open!

Some days later, a warm spring morning, he was standing at the door holding a burlap bag full of special food for Kasesa in his arms. Martin wasn't home and I had just made a useless attempt at starting a novel about a young woman who can't surrender herself to love because of a traumatic incident in her childhood.

Actually, I didn't recognize him. He had shaved his stubble and cut his curly hair short, was wearing a bright shirt, sleeves rolled up, a pair of prewashed prefaded jeans, and had an impertinent twinkle in his green-brown eyes that I hadn't noticed at our first meeting.

"Sorry if I'm interrupting," he said, "but I had to be in the neighborhood anyway, so I came to bring by something tasty for the new friend of the family so that it'll talk."

With an elegant movement he set the bag down in the hallway and acted as if he wanted to turn around and leave right away.

"Would you like something to drink?" I asked, still disconcerted by the sudden presence of this man, now so different, in my house.

"No, I'll be on my way again, I don't want to take up your

precious time. But, if it isn't inconvenient, would you mind if I had a look to see how Kasesa is doing?"

Still a bit worried that he might actually leave, I slipped behind him and closed the front door. Then, my discomposure hidden behind a self-assured gait, I repaired to the kitchen where the cockatoo jumped up on my shoulder from the countertop.

"Well, well, I see you two have already gotten acquainted with each other."

"Should I make some tea or coffee?"

He smiled shyly. "Coffee, please." He had a guilty expression on his face.

I was weak-willed with longing. He stood next to me, there were almost two feet between his arm and mine, and yet I felt his bushy arm burning against every centimeter of my skin. I inhaled the mixture of his overly sweet after-shave, the sweat of concealed shyness on his back, the fabric softener his wife had used to wash his bright shirt, the faint residue of coffee between his brushed shiny white teeth, the baby shampoo in his curly hair, cut too short, the sweet moisture of longing in his crotch. I yearned for his hands around my waist, between my thighs, but hoped, prayed, pleaded with my eyes that he would go quickly, without a handshake, without a kiss on the cheek, without goodbye, go and never come back. He stayed the whole day, was still there when Martin got home, stayed for dinner, stayed overnight at Martin's insistence, took a walk with us the following day through the dunes while Kasesa flew from his shoulder to mine, and disappeared that afternoon after a stand-up lunch of raw herring and fries, without any explanation or warning.

"I have to go. I'll call or write you both soon."

Suddenly spring was quiet, empty and dark again.

. . .

I dreamed orgasms, woke up surprised, as if someone had wiped in between my buttocks, wiped my vulva and my thoughts clean with a damp washcloth. Some of the dreams I can still remember, even though I didn't dare describe them in my diary.

Lotte and I, until she was eleven and I was ten, shared a sagging twin bed, in which we could do nothing but lie close together like spoons. Every night we would lightly tickle each other's bare backs until one of us would drift off during the pleasant stroking. There were also the restless nights, the long summer nights when the light sky, the sweltering heat, or the grown-ups' voices in the small back yards kept us awake. On those nights we would also lightly tickle each other's feet, legs and bottoms to the limit of surrender in all kinds of ways. While one was stroking, the other would tell a story. Lotte preferred to sing songs rather than make something up. I opted to fantasize.

Over a year ago Lotte confessed to me, after a bottle of champagne in celebration of her fortieth birthday, that when she couldn't sleep and I was lying beside her rolled up like a slug, my pillow over my head not under it, she would very sneakily pull down my pajama bottoms to see my shiny brown bottom with the short dark crack. That excited her, she said, that pretty deep groove and those small globes, smaller than her own.

I wasn't interested in hers. I got to see that while dressing and undressing every morning and every evening. But I do cherish the moments I never told anybody about and that I never understood myself.

We had each drawn squares with a stick in the black

trampled mud, nine or ten of them grouped in the shape of an airplane. Under the bushes in the loose earth we looked for large pebbles. I had a gray one the size of my fist, but as thin as a bread knife and as flat as a cutting board, that stayed exactly in the right place when I threw it at the airplane. No sidewalk had been laid yet, so I must have been five, maybe six, but certainly not seven. Lotte was seven and had already learned to read and write. She was better at hopscotch and even if she didn't find a flat stone in the bushes, her rock didn't bounce around when it was thrown, but landed precisely in the desired square. A few families had moved into the other row of houses. Ramona and her younger sister lived there. She was Indies, my age, but a head shorter, blonde, with café au lait skin and green eyes.

She was bad at hopscotch and she couldn't toss rocks, even if I gave her the best one, keeping one that wasn't as good for myself. Her little sister, who had gold curly hair tied back in a ponytail, like Ramona's, with a pink bow, the same light eyes, the same skin as Ramona's, jumped among us with both feet together in the same square. Only Ramona complained, "Yolanda, go away, you're much too little."

Lotte had won again for the thousandth time and was walking with Ramona to our back yard with the recently planted privet hedge to get a jump rope, because that was more fun, she said. I taught Yolanda to pay hopscotch. "Look, like this, no, not like that, like this."

She jumped ahead of me. She wore white ankle socks with black patent leather shoes, just like Ramona's, but half the size, that made no sound when she landed on the hard ground. She was a bouncing spring. The wide colorful summer dress flipped up high at each hop and exposed her white baggy underpants that were slightly drawn into the crack between her little buttocks, thereby covering them unevenly, smaller than a doll's, prettier, funnier than a doll's, because I traded Lotte my dolls for marbles that I would lose back to her in the next game. The plump little hands, dimples in both cheeks. The swinging of the ponytail at each failed hop. She skipped among the bushes.

"Are you looking for a rock?" I gave her mine, the big gray one.

She squatted down with a serious look on her face, sighed like a grown-up and pulled down her white panties.

"Do you have to pee? Yolanda, do you have to go wee-wee?"

She stepped out of her panties, partly, almost lost her balance, so I held her up and felt her little body. She squatted down again, her plump little arms out in front of her, her white panties clutched in her hands, while I looked on as a trickle of wet, very briefly and very weakly, appeared and made a little hollow in the loose black sand.

"Do you have to push, Yolanda?" I leaned over and searched the crack of her behind, my head to the side, to see the little dark hole that was hanging right above the ground close up. The stick with which I had drawn the hopscotch squares I carefully stuck between her white buttocks, letting it slide from top to bottom. She didn't move, remained in a squat while I moved the stick a few times gently, holding my breath, a little circle around her anus while softly pushing it with the end of the stick. I sniffed the stick, the dark odor of wood and earth, then smelled her behind, my nose against her crack, so that she fell forward and regarded me expectantly with questioning eyes.

I ran out of the bushes and never said hello to the child again, never played with her or her sister again, and very soon there were concrete tiles on the path, the road became asphalt and the bushes in the square had grown too thick to walk through.

· · ·

When I am overcome by desire, I am blind, greedy, untrust-
worthy, impatient, ruthless, without mercy.

When I found my clitoris, I also found an unseemliness that
I had until then never suspected of myself.

This morning, after I had already gotten up twice, once to
answer the phone and once to get something to drink, I
dreamed that I drowned the cockatoo in a fit of rage.

V

She is sitting at her dressing-table.

Hermanus van Maldegem, who made all the wooden furniture in the flat himself, also put together this dresser. Aunt Yossa has clambered up on the chair with the help of one of the many wooden footstools her father had nailed together and that are all over the house where light switches, the gas stove, faucets, coat racks, cupboards, doorknobs, the toilet pulley, are too high. She is sitting with her bottom on the edge of the yellow plastic seat and her feet resting on the stool. The large mirror with side panels that my Grandpa hung up crooked on the wall, shows her and me three times full-length. Twice a day she sits down in front of the dressing table and I sit on the edge of my Grandma's foldaway bed not to miss a single of my aunt's movements. The little compartments inside were adapted to Yossa's and my Grandma's needs. Behind the highest doors there are two brushes with seven different combs stuck into them, all kinds of hairpieces, in black, brown and gray for when the two women dress in sarongs and *kebayas*, put their hair up together with the falls into buns to make them look fuller, and lots of hairpins to poke through the buns, silver ones and gold ones, also ivory, on display in little boxes that fill the entire top portion of the dresser. The pins look dangerous. We're not allowed to touch them. The second tier, with the little doors that Aunt Yossa can open when she stands up, has a long narrow compartment on the inside of both of the doors in which twenty-eight little bottles of nail polish in shades ranging from mother-of-pearl to various tints of pink, orange, red, and even a few little bottles of lilac, almost purple, have been set out. There is also a little bottle of colorless varnish for Grandma's nails, because she prefers to cultivate her appearance in the colors that are, as she says, "natural." There is the same number of perfectly matching varieties of lipstick in a compartment below the nail polish, and on a little shelf beside some larger bottles there are some thirty-odd sample vials of perfume, eau de cologne and eau de toilette.

I'm allowed to smell each bottle and put some polish on the nails of my little fingers, not on all my fingers yet because I'm still too young. She briefly pats the fragrant powder puff on my forehead and cheeks. She has three different powders for her face: one daytime powder for summer and one for winter, and another one for parties. There is a black pencil for her eyebrows. The beautician removed not only Grandma's but Yossa's eyebrows completely and now every morning they each draw their favorite arc over each eye. Yossa in black. Grandma in brown.

At night before going to bed, freshly bathed, lilac-scented, bare forehead, shiny nose, her long hair brushed, her bare feet slipped into worn-out black beach clogs, the foot of her stiff leg at an angle, she takes out the nail polish that fits with the clothes she will wear to work the next day. From her little jewelry box she selects a necklace, a bracelet, rings and earrings to go along with the rest, and places her shoes under the chair with the plastic seat.

While she is telling us something about the office, she removes the color of that day from her long nails. Her boss was sick, a colleague had been a pain in the neck, somebody had had a birthday, or the day had been too long for the girl who brought coffee around so she had poured the coffee sloppily into the cups and spilled it on a letter that Aunt Yossa then had to retype.

She examines her nails, files a few edges, and discovers a little tear that she tries to fix with a colorless hardener. She waves her fingers in the air, blows on them, waves them, all the while talking about the past.

I sniff the nail polish remover and she says, "Don't do that, Meis, that isn't good for you, it'll make you stupid."

All of us children asked her, and not just once, either, but a few times to make sure. I heard my son ask as well, sitting in the same spot. The nails of his little fingers likewise colored, jiggling on the edge of Grandma Charlotte's bed, while she seemed to be flicking her long wrinkled fingers off; before that he had, just as I had done before, helped her burp and pass enough wind by scratching her back and at her request beating her shoulder blades and back with his little fists.

"Why are you so short?"

"Because I can't grow."

"Why can't you grow?"

"Because I was born that way."

"Why were you born that way?"

"Only God knows that. I'm sure he had his reasons."

"Why aren't you married?"

"Because I can't have any children."

"Why can't you have any children?"

"Because I was born that way."

"Didn't anybody want to marry you?"

"There was somebody. He always came to pick me up to go dancing, and he gave me a ring with a little diamond, but I didn't accept it."

"Why not?"

"I said, 'You'd be better off marrying a normal woman.' He may have thought that he was in love, but I would always have thought that he chose me out of pity."

"Did he marry a normal woman?"

"He died in the war."

Everybody had a good time on my fortieth birthday party except me. Even the cockatoo, a year ago still with its former owner, was having fun with Aunt Manda, whom it hadn't let out of its sight since she had arrived, and with whom it flapped around above the dance floor despite the bustle and loud music. Although it would sometimes gnaw at our wooden furniture when strangers were over, it now seemed to be singing along with the dancing guests.

I tried not to let my apathy show. The only way, it seemed to me, was to dance myself empty, move to the rhythm of the bass, and let my shoulders, stomach and hips follow the melody, my arms and hands ready to glide with each surprising riff played by the sax or trumpet player. Then the laughter and the joy would come of their own accord. I forgot that he hadn't wanted to come, that what I took to be true love was no less, but certainly no more, than the mistake I had made earlier in my life with Martin, who watched me now and then from a distance and wouldn't be deceived by the lively swaying of my hips and stomach throughout the long evening and then the long night until the quiet early morning.

• • •

"What does 'in love' mean, Aunt Yossa?"

"That you think about somebody all day long."

"Were you in love with that man?"

"What man?"

"The man that died."

"Yes, of course I was, but I've been in love lots of times."

"Does it feel bad to be in love?"

"Without love, life isn't worthwhile, Meisje."

For weeks at a time he came over three, maybe five times a week and usually spent the night. After that first visit I initially tried to avoid him. I'd shut myself in my workroom with the excuse that I was busy working on my new novel, but wouldn't put a word down on paper. Martin and he went through all our bookcases with a fine-tooth comb for interesting poets. Martin knew of more poets that he did, many Asian poets, from India, Bangladesh, Nepal and Tibet, of whom Neo had never heard. He knew a lot of French, Spanish and Portuguese poems by heart. They quoted snippets of poetry that appealed to them. Now and then I'd open the door to my workroom a crack to listen in on their conversations. Already during the second visit, I must have fallen asleep on the mattress in my workroom, Martin showed him poems that I had written for him with a drawing pen on handmade paper sewn into a binding finished off with a brown suede cover (I had cut the leather from Martin's old jacket that he had worn when I first got to know him).

Twenty poems. Each poem was an expression of one year with Martin, sober in imagery, and veiling neither pain nor excitement. I had never meant them for other eyes than Martin's, didn't know whether I should feel hurt or flattered when at breakfast Neo Pecoque said that he had never in his life been so moved by poetry, while he drew the little book that Martin had given him the previous night for bedtime reading out of the breast pocket of his jacket.

Martin was in the shower and we were stacking up the breakfast dishes and muesli bowls when he laid his hand on my shoulder and whispered, his voice hoarse, "May I be your muse from now on?"

I had a fight with Martin after he left two days later, after he and Martin had been making plans for days to encourage me to write more verse that Neo wanted to publish as a collector's edition in cooperation with the artist of the plucked cockatoo.

We took a walk out on the sandy heath and pine woods of the Veluwe. Neo and Martin laughed a lot and at each plant, tree, bird or fleeting hare, recited a line that was appropriate, at which the other had to guess who the poet was. They became peevish; mutilated and improved the verses as it suited them.

I observed their bodies as they walked ahead of me, then stood still, slapping each other on the back like old school chums, or grinned like naughty children, sitting beside each other on the trunk of a sawed down tree.

Martin, tall, dark blond with graying temples, tanned skin, broad shoulders, still slim despite his forty-three years, inspired respect when he was serious, and was charming when he laughed.

Neo, pale, freckles on and around his nose, short, too paunchy around the waist, his jeans with a brown leather belt pulled up too high, always seemed to be beaming. He was not a good-looking man, but he fascinated me; his voice just a little too loud, his dark green eyes sparkling, his glasses first on, then off, his mouth laughing continually, and sometimes, seeing a crushed frog, a little pile of pheasant feathers or a broken red poppy, he was almost shy all of a sudden, his mouth small and closed.

I had never been in love with an ugly man. They had all had athletic or slightly lanky bodies, were tall and powerful, or short and slim, robust or sensitive, but had always been perfect. Neo, at thirty-five, with the looks of somebody around fifty, didn't know how to dress, his stomach was too fat and from a distance his short neck on the slightly stooped back with the drooping shoulders lent him the aspect of a dwarf.

I saw him, and yet I saw nothing. I wandered behind the two men, and possibly, that's what I think now many months later, I was really happy only on that particular walk.

Grandma, I don't know why everything that I felt with this man was so much more intense. I didn't want to let it happen. I had been living for certainly two years, or in any case a year and a half, faithful to Martin and faithful to myself, with Martin as my sole intimate lover.

I dare to write only you, only now, now that I know that you will have forgotten this sentence while you are reading it, about how I really always tried to keep every man away, but how I seemed to be the victim of an instinct in myself that I couldn't master, like the woman's Kasesa in the legend, of another self that would risk everything for a single sensation that seemed more important than food, a part of myself that seemed to go its own way. Martin thinks that for ten years already, maybe even longer, I have permitted only him to touch my body and, in fact, things were going really well, Grandma, there was so much peace in me. I thought I had achieved something, that the last incidents had really only been mistakes in order to realize even better that I wasn't seeking out those kinds of experiences anymore. I wrote my girl friend, "I cringe at the thought that I would ever get involved with somebody other than Martin, because I want Martin, only him, him only."

I did occasionally see a man and think, "How does he feel, how does he kiss, what would it be like spending a month in Tibet with him, or a few nights in Manhattan?" But my curiosity was no longer enough to break up what Martin and I had managed to foster after twenty years of trial and error.

In my books, however, I fantasized more and more about love with many others, to such an extent that Martin advised me to put a little less sexuality in my books because it distracted from the real themes. We exchanged words about this. As a consequence of the discussions with Martin, I withdrew my last manuscript from the publisher when the text was already being set by the printer. In our talks I blamed Martin for not being able, as my husband, to cope with the fact that my work was so frankly sensual, but in my thoughts I was having another dialogue with him, and I let him win our heated discussions. He doesn't know that I took back my manuscript, although he may suspect now. I'm glad that Martin is so critical of my work, but at the same time I don't trust his motives.

Martin would be furious if he were to read this. He is convinced of his objectivity and says he is one of the few people capable of analyzing my work without confusing the contents with me as a person.

We both waved Neo off as if he were going to be away for a long time and were not going to be standing on our doorstep as soon as the day after tomorrow, or in any case, the following week. We hadn't gotten back into the house before I heard myself say, my voice as stringent as a schoolmarm's, "Why did you let him read those poems?"

(It was as if with that question I wanted to make Martin responsible for the screaming longing to embrace that strange man, who was driving out of the street in his ostentatious car, my head in the pit of his arm, my arms around his soft waist, his freckled nose in my hair.

Everything I said was meant to heap upon Martin the guilt that I was feeling.)

I can see his face, frowning eyebrows, light eyes with the black pupils so small in those blue irises, and I forget, while I am throwing "our intimacies" and "personal love poems" in his face like swear words loud enough for the neighbors to hear, that I love him, more than anybody else, before, now and ever.

Moments later, near the kitchen table, where earlier Neo had still been touching my shoulder and where for a couple of seconds, to my own horror, I had wished Martin dead, Martin says, his face filled with earnest regret, "I thought you liked the idea. You adore that fancy edition of his, and your poems are something to be proud of. It's great if he does something with them, isn't it?"

"It's our little book. They are love poems about our difficult years and our happy years together. You don't just let anybody read them, do you?"

"Neo isn't just anybody."

(Here I had the chance to warn Martin of my fear for myself, the shame of longing for that man. I should have admitted to Martin, "Exactly." But I kept my mouth shut.)

When Neo called that same evening and I answered the phone, he said, his voice husky again and passionate, "Melanie, I want to call you Meisje, just like Martin does, is that permissible?"

"Everybody calls me Meisje, even my son."

"Meisje, please, answer me, you only have to say yes or no, may I be your muse?"

I was pressing the receiver tightly against my ear to prevent Martin's catching any of his words.

Without a sound I replaced the receiver and stared off. There is still a way back, I thought.

Suddenly Martin was standing beside me, his large warm

hand on my back, his familiar voice, "I can see that he's in love with you, but in these twenty years he hasn't been the first one. That doesn't have to be an obstacle to a friendship. He's a fascinating character, he makes me laugh a lot, especially when he raps one of Verlaine's poems, or when he recites John Lennon like Shakespeare."

"I don't know what to make of him."

Kasesa flew around the room wildly and with a lot of clamor landed on the table, next to the phone. We followed the bird's movements. It clawed at the apparatus with its foot.

"I can see how you lighten up when he's around. Yesterday you laughed all day."

Kasesa, having knocked the receiver off the hook, raised its crest and became restless when the soft buzz changed over to the busy signal.

"Yeah, he's funny," I tried to say as indifferently as possible, "it's as if I've known him for years."

As I replaced the receiver, I added, "And he gets along well with Kasesa, because I do have to get used to all the attention that a free bird like that needs."

Martin, who was hereby reminded that Kasesa could use a bath, lifted the cockatoo, who disliked being picked up by him, off the table, and before he went upstairs to the bathroom with the creature said, "I invited him to Aunt Yossa's birthday party. I thought it would be nice for him to go to one of your family get-togethers, and your aunt will fall for him, I'm sure of it."

She too, coy when she went down the street wearing a hat and matching gloves, impish when she was teaching me how to box, "Don't just punch with your right, use your left, too, Meisje," flying through the air from uncle to uncle to my father who'd toss her up towards the ceiling and catch her again just above the floor, and making eyes, being provocative, playful when she let her favorite music resound through the speakers and encourage every man, woman and child to dance, was an example for me.

Dreams in which I am child again hardly ever take place at my parents' home, but almost always at Grandpa and Grandma van Maldegem's.

Every friend had at some point been brought to Grandma Charlotte's house to be checked out by Aunt Yossa.

"Ooh, Meis, what sexy eyebrows he has. And, *adú!* What muscles, his arms were simply made to bite into. . . ."

Only when she was contentedly rubbing her upper arms and pleasantly pursing her lips as if she were delighting in one of the Indonesian sweets my father used to bake for her, did I admit to being in love. With a gleam in her eye, Aunt Yossa had a way of leaning over toward me to ask, "Do you sometimes see that good-looking Italian anymore, that Don Juan, oh what was his name, Claudio wasn't it, oh what a charming young man he was."

Even the men with whom I spent time when Martin and I had already been married for many years, and our son regularly stayed overnight at Grandpa and Grandma van Maldegem's, I introduced to Aunt Yossa. She would wink at me as she handed me the tray with the black Tobruk-style coffee and win over the newcomer sitting across from her with her colorful stories and her engaging smile.

The radio was always on. When the news started, she would turn it off and play records. In some way or other she sensed which music was the new guest's favorite, and because even after Grandpa's death she still went to the record store every week to hear what new things had come out and choose something. She had, besides Hawaiian and Indonesian *kronchong* music, a varied collection of pop and jazz, including Bob

Dylan, Stevie Wonder, Bill Haley, Joe Cocker, Glenn Miller, Miles Davis, Dizzy Gillespie, Stan Getz, even Chick Corea. She also had some classical music, including particularly Mozart, Ravel's *Bolero* of course, and a few operas like *Carmen* because Grandma Charlotte liked "*L'Amour est un oiseau rebel*" so much.

When I leaned down to embrace her and say goodbye, she would say, "You're both going out to have a nice time before you go home I'm sure. Enjoy! And give my best to Martin."

Grandma, every day in your house was fascinating. There was no bickering like there was at home between my parents, there was music. When Aunt Yossa was at the office I enjoyed the quiet with the birds singing in the dining room, I poked around in the house, and every corner was like an exciting book full of adventures.

My son liked being with you both. But he talks about the birds, how Grandpa fed one of the birds from his mouth, and talked sternly to another one and never let it out of the cage. He talks about the walk with Grandpa down to the pet store, about the little cigarettes that Grandpa smoked on the sly in the storage shed because Grandma had forbidden him to smoke on account of his hawking fits every morning, and how a fire had broken out and the neighbors had called the fire department because of the smoke coming out from under the shed door. He still knows about the moving of the cages. Each cage had a place for the morning and another for the night. And yet he was only four when Grandpa died, and the birds ended up with Uncle Didi in his room-sized aviary. Whenever they went out the door together, they both had caps on. No matter what the weather, he would choose one of the many caps from Grandpa's coatrack.

The day began, for him as well, with breakfast that we were allowed to prepare ourselves with the help of a considerable choice of both sweet and savory things to put on white bread, gray government bread or brown bread, and sometimes as a treat, the white sticky rice with melted Javanese cane sugar and coconut. Afterward we each washed our own dishes and silverware and set them in the dish rack. In the meantime I could hear you doing the wash in the bathroom. Even when I myself had a washing machine for my son's diapers, you still washed everything by hand because you thought machines and electricity were a nuisance. Meanwhile Aunt Yossa would be sitting in front of the dressing table. My cousins went to the shed downstairs with Grandpa, after he retired, to clean the bird cages, feed the birds or walk him to the post office. When he was still working at the bank they would get up as early as he did, bring him to the tram, wave him off and play soccer in the street, or build huts from junk wood out in what was called "The Field," the barren terrain where a fire station came to be located years later.

I would sit beside Aunt Yossa and study her as, with a steady hand, she would draw her sleepy face awake again. I would carry her bag, big and heavy I recall, and my other hand would be tightly held in hers. First, carefully down the portico steps, then down the steps to the stoop. She always wore gloves, even in the summer, and every third step she would say, "*Awas, Meisje, careful.*" Lotte never wanted to come along to bring her to the office. She thought it was scary, those looks on people's faces when she walked with her down the street. Maybe I had a problem with that too, but I felt it was my duty to escort her and wanted to be just as brave as she was, seemingly impervious to the jeering of children and the prying eyes.

At the end of the day I'd pick her up again. I would stand at the big entrance and among the hundreds of people leaving the building see two other little Lilliputian ladies, who were taller than Aunt Yossa, come out, but they weren't as pretty because they had misshapen and puffed up heads, not movie-star faces like my aunt's.

She took the time on her way both to and from the office to greet warmly people she knew. The mail carrier would double over like a jackknife. I thought he was in love with her, but I was fourteen when I discovered that she would give him a hefty tip every time he came to the door of their apartment to drop off the mail when it was too big for the mailbox beside the outside portico door.

She greeted the man at the dry cleaner's with a beaming smile, even just after being abusively addressed as a dirty old peanut troll by a little boy. The pharmacist would rush out in his white doctor's jacket to wave at her, and with him would come the aroma of twenty kinds of licorice and spicy candies. And the lady from the lingerie shop who was still closed at this early hour would tap on the inside of the window, draw the lace curtain to one side just a bit and magically produce a smile on her sour-looking face.

There were some tram drivers who would ring and wave, but I didn't know whether they really meant it in a friendly manner, or whether they, like so many others, would have shouted at her or stood staring out of curiosity if they hadn't had their handy bell to show that they had caught sight of her striking person. There were gentlemen on bicycles who tipped their hats to her in passing. She always greeted them wholeheartedly in return, "Hello, Mr. van Slooten," "Good morning, Mr. van der Laan," "How are things, Mr. Verstraete."

"Is that your niece, Miss van Maldegem?"

"Yes, this is Meisje, the daughter of a younger sister of mine, Meisje Fleurie."

I fought my rage at the big boys who stood at tramstops waiting and throwing bricks at us, pointing at my aunt, whooping in theatrical howls, threatening in shouts to beat her up. Aunt Yossa, who had each evening together with Grandpa taught us boxing and the Indonesian martial art, *pentjak silat*, on the rolled out mattresses, said, "Act as if you don't hear a thing, Meisje, we have to accept things as they are." She could feel the growing fury in my hand and almost had to crush my fingers to force me to calm down.

But when, a moment later, some well-dressed gentleman, Indo or Dutch, it didn't matter, got off his bicycle and removed his hat and shook my aunt's hand with a slight bow, with the words, "Hello, Miss Fleurie, are you taking good care of your aunt?" I knew, at six, seven years old, that I wanted to learn particularly my aunt's poise in the face of her disability, her proud gait.

"Tell us again about before," we said, shiny from the soap, in the new baby doll nighties we had been allowed to choose at the lingerie shop that afternoon after Grandma had gone with us to pick Aunt Yossa up from the office. The shop with the lace curtains where the lady with the angry face lifts Aunt Yossa up on a tall stool, coat off, gloves off, as if we're visiting, after which the other lady, her sister or something, who also had an angry face, but friendlier eyes, whispering, pulls all kinds of bras and underwear out of boxes and plastic packaging. "The very latest, Miss van Maldegem, we just got it in this morning, you'll just love it. . . ."

As a last request, when there was already a pile of underwear lying beside the cash register, Aunt Yossa or Grandma asked, "Would you have something new for the girls, too?" Cotton pajamas, a see-through night gown, a lace slip, or—and we had to laugh at the word, so we said, "Just normal pajamas," but Grandma replied, "You have to move with the times"—a baby doll nightie.

· · ·

"I always had to baby-sit my younger brothers and sisters, and I get spanked if the little ones cry because they fell down, or if they fight amongst themselves. Because I happen to be the oldest. I have a cane with which I keep the others under control, but I hardly ever have to use the cane. I only have to call out, or to look, hard like this, with my eyes, and they already listen to me.

"At school I always have fun. I put thumbtacks on Miss Ra. . . Raaymakers. . . Razemaaier. . . no Raads. . . Raas. . . oh what's her name again, blonde with glasses, a tall beanpole with no breasts. She sends me down the hall to the headmistress, a strict nun, but I climb into this tree, a. . . uh. . . you know, those nuts with the soft shells, oval-shaped, in clusters and on the inside they're hard, tsk, those ones that if you bump them they fall, but then they're ripe already. When I'm sitting up in the tree I can't eat them, they aren't good yet.

"Nobody saw me. I break the uh. . . *kenari, kenari* it's called, I break this big *kenari* nut from the branch and, *tuar!* right in through the open window, at the skinny beanpole. At first I don't hit her, but I do hit the blackboard. You can hear "clunk." She looks up, but doesn't see me. My girl friends have already spotted me, of course they giggle. Then I throw another one, and another one, *tuar!* until I hit her, then I stay still. *Adú!* I have to write a thousand lines for punishment and she hits me on the knuckles with a ruler. We also get taught by Sister Aafje. *Kassian*, actually a sweet woman, that nun. She's always giving me compliments. "Good for you, Yossa," and "Follow Yossa's example." I shoot crumpled bits of paper when she's writing on the blackboard. She has such a fat behind, sticks out a bit, just like a duck. We call her The Penguin. I aim at her big butt with my slingshot, but she can't feel anything through all her clothes, you see. During recess I saw the legs of her chair halfway through. Only two of the legs, not

all four. But when she sits down I can't help laughing. So I
give myself away. She hasn't even fallen through the chair yet
and I'm already being punished. But I'd rather be punished
than pitied."

"You never know. . . Yossa. She was strong. . . just ask your
mother, or Divette, she'll be able to remember that too, I'm sure,
she wasn't afraid of anything. When we had just gotten out of
the Japanese camp my mother was. . . well. . . it bothers me to
think about that. . . because my older brother was dead, we'd
only just heard. Actually we were happy to be out of the camp,
and then you hear such an awful piece of news. . . . Rotten for
my mother, of course. Before the war, my brother was always
showing off with her, because he was big for his age and he
looked older, and then he'd have Ma on his arm and he was
proud when they thought that she was his girl. . . oh. . . and he
was a Don Juan, my brother. . . he was always saying, 'With one
beauty on your arm you win a lot of sweethearts.' He had a lot
of girlfriends, usually older than he was, even though he wasn't
anywhere near seventeen yet. His friends all came to our house,
and that's why there were always lots of boys after us. . . . They
were brought by my brother. When the war broke out he had
to go to the men's camp and we never saw him again. Momma
had announced everywhere that she still hadn't received news of
Poppa and my brother, although she had already picked up our
youngest brother from Surabaya. Oh, how skinny he was, and
his eyes, so hollow. He stared at us, and didn't listen. Then that
friend my brother used to have came by, a really nice boy. . . a
blond Indo, and he said, 'Mrs. van Maldegem, where is your
husband, I have something to tell him.' Yossa said, 'Poppa isn't
back yet. We still haven't gotten information on where he is, and
we don't know anything about my brother, either.' 'Mrs. van

Maldegem,' he said, 'forgive me, I don't want to tell you this, but I have to. He was the bravest of us all. I wasn't in his barracks, or else I would have held him back. You know, he had William of Orange's well-known motto *je maintiendrai* tattooed on his chest, he had always been rebellious anyway. He didn't let them lay down the law for him. They. . . ugh. . . so badly. . . we all had to watch. . . .'

"Such a shame, that young man, that he had to come and tell us, I can still see him standing there, he was so skinny and now he was shaking. My mother wouldn't eat anymore, only sleep. She had already dreamed it, she said, he had appeared while she was sleeping and had said, 'Momma, things are fine with me, keep going, be strong.' Then my little brother took to the road. And he won't listen to us. Then there's that sound of the phone poles, when the *rampokkers* pound on them with their sticks. Then we keep still, huddle together and wait till they've passed by. But the sound stopped right near our house. That's when we noticed that my little brother wasn't at home. Oh, I don't ever want to think about it again. Yossa pulls little bamboo slats down from here and there, an itty bitty stick, and she runs out because she thinks they are hurting my brother. I can hear her scream, very loud, like this 'aaaaaaaaauuuuuuuuuuuuuuoooooooow.' And I think, soon there will only be five of us left. . . if Yossa and my little brother get skewered by the bayonets. It is so quiet, so quiet, and your mother, Emma, she wants to go outside, to see, she can be furious, your mother. She wants to fight. I hold her back. 'Don't, Em, otherwise Momma will be left with only three daughters, because they'll kill you, too, what are you trying to do?' She must have a guardian angel, Yossa, I always thought that maybe she got more angels because our dear Lord regretted having made her so small.

"We can see her come back in with our little brother. Her face is angry and she drags him in. Angry at *him*, she is, she yells at him, 'Come here, you, inside with you, how many times have I told you to listen to me,' and the *rampokkers* let her go on her way. He had been surrounded and they had already started making him sweat.

"Then we heard the phone poles again. They were moving on. Another house. Then I'm glad. Lucky, they're far away, not near us anymore. But Yossa had us gather up a bundles of clothes and toilet articles and as soon as the sun was up, go back to the camp. It was safer there. Yossa prodded Momma into action. 'You've got other children. Life goes on.'

"That's just the way Yossa is."

There was a lot of fighting in your street, Grandma, especially on The Field, that empty lot with huts both above and below the ground and the secret tunnels running underneath that were forbidden by the police and our parents because of the risk of collapse, but which seemed absolutely essential for stashing the bicycle chains, the stilettos and the brass knuckles, weapons without which my cousins wouldn't have felt safe. They weren't used, but since the Indo boy from two doors down had caught the Dutch boys on the street with those kinds of objects, my cousins had swapped their stamp collection (stamps that had been soaked off the many letters that Didi had sent to Aunt Manda when he had been in the navy) with the oldest boy of the opposition for street fighters' materiel to defend their huts.

In one of those self-made huts on The Field, where us girls would be invited when there was a lull to play house with our cousins in the dark crowded space on your old batik and *ikat* bedspreads (the boys had nabbed them from your dresser) with ever so many good-night-Meises and good-night-Mannies, a few kisses and an intimate embrace that lasted for minutes, followed by good-morning-Meis and good-morning-Mannie, more kisses on my face and then "I'm going to the office now," or "I'm off," "Bye Mannie," "Bye Meis, see you later." The Indo neighbor boy with the Chinese eyes and the full lips wanted to be my doctor.

"But I'm not sick," I said stubbornly.

"Yes you are, you've got a stomach ache."

"No, I don't."

"Yes you do, let me take a look."

While the others were off scouting, bloodthirstily itching for a reason to fight with the other inhabitants of The Field, I let him lift up my summer dress and feel around my stomach.

"Where does it hurt?"

"It doesn't hurt."

"Does it hurt here?" his voice soft.

I nodded, let his hand rove. This warmth was even hotter than the ribbon.

I was a little older, maybe there weren't any huts on The Field anymore and they'd already put up barbed wired because a child had suffocated in one of the tunnels, but it was fall because there were a lot of gold and brown leaves on the steps, blown over onto our walk from the square near the little houses for the elderly. There weren't very many flowerpots on the balcony anymore, and I was there for the weekend without cousins, even without Lotte because she was in the hospital to have her tonsils out.

From the balcony I looked up the street and saw how he, his black bristly hair, his dark blue jacket over gray polyester pants, was surrounded by half a dozen boys, all just as big as he was.

The fattest one punched him in the stomach and as he was try-ing to block the punch the way I had also learned from Aunt Yossa to avoid a blow, another one, dressed in shorts despite the cool weather, shoved him from behind so he lost his balance and almost tripped. I didn't wait to see anymore. I didn't think twice. I was Aunt Yossa, the way Aunt Manda had told me she was. I jumped off the balcony, it was only the first floor, and landed on the steps in front of the portico door, as I had done quite a few times playing hide-and-seek. I was still about fifty yards from the fight, but shrieking loudly, whooping Wild West Indian whoops, I stormed at them with two *sapulidis* that I had snatched from the corner of Grandma's balcony, one in each hand. I must have surprised them sufficiently with my shouting and the two unfamiliar Indonesian brooms. They took off. But he scrambled to his feet, insulted, and said, "I could have handled them by myself, too, you know."

(He never came up to my Grandma's with my cousins after that and I would look towards the street when I walked the sidewalk in front of their portico.)

Aunt Yossa was cheerful, beamed, walked dancing, singing or whistling through the house with a mischievous look in her black eyes, always made fun of herself, was the first to laugh at her own faults; but these past years she has had regular pe-riods of depression because, as she says herself, she not only has to remember her own memories, but also yours.

Yet, she still eagerly talks to everyone, still arranges with her acquaintances and friends for the both of you to go out to the seniors' exercise group, bingo or Indonesian parties and re-unions three times a week. Neither of you can walk outside anymore. For you it's too risky, the wind is too harsh, or it's too warm so you might perspire and catch cold, or it's raining or snowing. And now that you've both been robbed three times, once out in the street, twice at home, Aunt Yossa doesn't want to go out by herself anymore, either.

"It's not that I'm afraid," she says, "but I'm powerless."

Three brown boys, "I think North Africans, by their accents," threatened her, not even a hundred yards from the portico, at ten o'clock in the morning. "A long thin knife," she said, "like one of those. . . what're they called that people used to cut down the *alang alang* in Indonesia."

Once back home, without her handbag, having lost her billfold, her cards, checks and her hospital ID card, since she had been on her way to the pharmacy for blood pressure pills, she hadn't wanted to upset you, so she sat down on the wooden stool in the bathroom, still shaking, and cried. Only after she had calmed down did she call the neighbor, a nice Dutch man who also gives her a hand when she can't get the water heater going, or if something's wrong with the heating. He had the police come. You were gruff because you couldn't understand what the man in uniform was doing in your house, and so the officer wouldn't understand, although with obvious signs of annoyance, you kept asking Yossa about it in Malayan, until she finally said, "I was robbed on the street."

"Only robbed? They didn't try anything? Luckily, as long as you're not hurt. Material loss isn't a loss."

You turned on the television and with the help of the remote control clicked until you found a soccer game.

The second time similar types came and stood beside your beds. You had woken up, but by the time they'd left, you had already forgotten the incident, "Why did you go and make such a mess, Yossa," you queried with irritation, while Auntie was still sitting on the couch, white as a sheet, still sobbing from fear, smoking one cigarette after another, and staring at the chaos.

With her temples throbbing, she had been forced to watch as a gang of four still young boys had smashed the old record player that she had never gotten rid of so she could play her favorite 78s, against the wall because it was "worthless." Grandpa had bought it for her over forty years before upon arriving in The Netherlands, because she couldn't find her niche in this cold country, was homesick for Jakarta and her friends, and couldn't find work since, as she was told at each job interview, "You don't have to work, you can get disability here." A lot of the black vinyl records they broke in two with karate cries until they got bored and one of them discovered the VCR that Aunt Yossa had gotten from the family for her previous birthday but had never wanted to take out of the box, tucked under a closet. After that they had hurried off with the VCR, the entertainment center and the big collection of LPs, sorted by styles into special suitcases of white, dark red and gray leatherette. The third time you were both staying at my mother's to recover from this last incident, and this time they made such a mess, including roughly dumping out and plundering the dressing table in their search for secret compartments, that Aunt Yossa couldn't figure out anymore what she was missing. Totally desolate, she let you both be put on a waiting list for a two-room apartment in a retirement residence.

"Why?" You had asked, "I live fine here, why do I have to move? I've always lived here."

(It must be wonderful to be able to forget, Grandma, to be able, like you, to sum up fifty years of marriage in a single sentence, "I had a good man, really, very good, but nobody's perfect, and in the end we all die.")

Aunt Yossa's birthday, her seventieth, would be the last party in the apartment where all my dreams still take place.

. . .

When you're in love, everything happens by itself. You don't notice how much time you spend in front of the mirror and that you've changed clothes seven times before you go out the door.

The day is never too long, it isn't you dancing, dancing all day, and you don't tire. The moon always seems full, even when it's new.

Yesterday for my birthday party I initially chose the dress I had worn to Aunt Yossa's seventieth birthday party, the dress Neo always said was Cinderella's ball gown and which he kept asking me to wear for him alone.

I felt like a little bird in a pheasant feather suit.

Of course I received compliments, possibly well-intentioned, but I took the dress off again and put on something else, something gray with brown. Martin even said, "Please, do it for me, you're so beautiful in that dress."

But the dress is past.

When I was still too little to go to the office with Aunt Yossa, I would listen, after waving Auntie off from the balcony, to the sounds in the bathroom. The slightest change in tempo, water sloshing a little more or a little less, the slurping of the drain, the smell of chlorine, each signal was an indication of how long it would take before you hung the wash out to dry on the back balcony. The wash that had to be bleached in cast iron buckets we were allowed to push down with long bleached-white ladles when it ballooned up from time to time. You went to bathe yourself on the wooden rise beside the porcelain basin you had meanwhile run full of cold water, and out of the corner of my eye, supposedly busy with the ladles and the soaking wash in the buckets, I observed you.

You were so much paler than my mother, had bigger breasts,

a bigger stomach, and you washed yourself so much more vigorously. With both arms above your head you threw pails of cold water over your soap-covered body. Your feet in the black clogs with the rubber straps. Those clogs were also in our bathroom, under the sink, but were never used. In your slip you sat down at the dressing table. Standing up, a bare foot on the plastic seat of the wooden chair, you put Nivea first on your face, then your neck and arms, and lastly on your legs. Ready just in time for morning exercises on the radio, you did the prescribed exercises in your slip, with next door in the living room, the fast piano music loud.

Thereupon we would all choose your dress for the day out of one of the many closets. Grandpa would have gone to the bank hours before. He left earlier than Aunt Yossa and kissed us goodbye when we were still asleep, his cap on, summer or winter, the visor bumping my forehead, his prickly chin against my cheek, his mouth smelling of tobacco.

"No, not from that closet, Lotte, those dresses are for going out."

"So let's go out, Grandma."

"Good, then we'll all go on a canal-boat ride."

Everything that was fun we did with Grandma. The canal boats, the Artis zoo, the park, shopping at the street market, puppet shows, the movies where Grandma would stand tirelessly in line with us for all the movies with Conny and Rex, Conny and Peter, Cliff Richard, and especially with Elvis Presley in them, and then we'd eat french fries and meatball snacks at a little lunch counter place; she even accompanied us to pop concerts when we were still too young to go alone. She took us to *West Side Story* and lied about our ages. My first bra, my first bikini, my first petticoat, my first wash and set, my first perm, my first pumps, my first minidress, even my first maxipads I got from her.

. . .

"Should I let go of my prejudices against our Southern neighbors?" asked my son. He was sweating from dancing rock 'n roll with Lotte, and had also danced a foxtrot with you, very awkwardly, and in so-doing, I suspect, stepped on your toes many a time. "What an amusing Fleming you two brought along. And a fancy-looking Cadillac Eldorado convertible, almost as old as you, mother-dear. That's the toy car model I always wanted, but you all thought it was too pricey, so I got a plastic Tonka truck from Martin instead."

"You mean that big pink one parked up on the curb? Is that a Cadillac? How do you know it's his?"

He shook his head in pity.

"All my life I've known that you don't know the first thing about car models, but that you don't know that Belgians have different licence plates disappoints me."

When the dress had been selected, Grandma let us pick the right shoes to go with it. With a dress that was blue and beige, I chose a blue pair and Lotte chose a beige. Grandma pointed out the dark green leaves that could also be found in the fabric. "What do you think of black?" Or she would point out the white background that came out especially in the short sleeves and around the bust, and at the row of white buttons which closed the dress up the front like a coat. "White goes well with white, and look, the sun's shining, we're going out, so white shoes with a very small heel are very appropriate now."

From a higher cupboard, for which she had to climb up on a chair, she took a blue sunhat with a white ribbon, secured a beige silk rose under the white ribbon, put a touch of color on her lips, so that it only seemed as if she were a lot happier now, pinned a black-green brooch on the left side of her dress, took out her blue handbag and said, "We're going, girls."

At the door Lotte would ask, "Grandma, can I wear a hat, too?"

And then we'd go downstairs to the room where Aunt Yossa always slept when Grandpa was still alive. The French doors were open a crack. "Take your pick," said Grandma as she opened the big closet beside the foldaway bed. The scent of camphor and secrets stunned me. We poked around all the shelves; in boxes, in plastic bags, wrapped in tissue paper, there lay hundreds of hats, or so it seemed. I looked until I found a straw hat, blue like Grandma's, with a pink ribbon and a brooch with little lilac forget-me-nots pinned onto the ribbon that was frayed here and there and gray with dust.

Lotte took out a dark green hat with feathers, a peacock's, said Grandma, and a pastel veil.

"That's actually for evening wear, in the winter, for a fancy dinner like Christmas or New Year's," said Grandma, but that didn't matter, thought Lotte. She turned around in front of the mirror, changed the veil around, put it up on the hat, or hung it in front of her face, studied hersef in the slightly too large hat that sat down below her eyebrows so that the veil covered her face and neck when it hung down, until Grandma said, "Are you ready?"

Only then did Lotte ask, "Grandma, may we please put on some lipstick too?"

I didn't want any make-up, but watched how Lotte refused Grandma's help and exceeded her lips with bright pink.

"Come on," said Grandma. "*Ayó!* Or else we'll be too late for the movie.

· · ·

115

Of course Neo stole everybody's heart. The party seemed to have been arranged especially for him. Right after our arrival, while I was still greeting everyone, Aunt Manda came over to me and whispered in my ear, "Who's that Belgian anyway? How did you get to know him? What a charmer!" Family had come from every corner of the world and every corner of the apartment was being utilized. Even the downstairs, which Yossa and Grandma hadn't used for years because walking the stairs had become too much of a strain, Aunt Manda had arranged as a dance and smoking room because of the French doors that opened onto the little patio. Children had been posted to keep out unwanted guests, but the children encouraged the younger neighbors to have something to drink, or at least to get into the swing of the disco music on Aunt Manda's granddaughter's boombox that was blaring out over the other back yards and inner courtyard. Upstairs in the dining room a band made up of elderly ladies and gentlemen played *kronchong* and Hawaiian music. The Indo neighbor boy, who hadn't been living two doors away anymore for ages but out on the polder with his Dutch wife in a newly built-up town, who still had Chinese eyes and full lips, but was now half bald, graying and fat, mostly fat, was sitting behind the drumset, the youngest member of the band. He greeted me with his eyebrows, wrinkles on his forehead.

For the first time I saw Yossa's many girl friends all at the same time. But somebody had died, somebody I knew well, whom I'd seen once kissing another girl friend on the sofa, a big Dutch gray one who's still alive. She had worn flat brown tied shoes, party or no party, this time too, sitting on her lap. At first they hadn't seen me, but then they were startled that I was standing there watching them and the big gray one said, "I thought everybody was downstairs." (All of us were, in fact, on the back patio, but I had come upstairs to pee and wanted to grab a cookie out of the cookie tin because I was hungry.)

Not the dark one with the puffy cheeks and little curls, she died a long time ago, long before Grandpa. I'd seen Aunt Yossa cry that time, although I'd forgotten that Aunt Yossa could cry because she cried only when she thought we weren't looking. The other dark one, who's dead now, the one that drove the red Morris, had comforted her. They had also kissed, and this girl friend had stroked Aunt Yossa's long thick black hair, but they weren't startled when they saw that I was looking at them. Lung cancer, euthenasia a few days before with the emphatic wish that Aunt Yossa's party be held anyway, "Because I'll be there, you know, in spirit," she had said.

Aunt Yossa put a plate of *nasi kuning* out on the balcony for her, otherwise she might feel she hadn't been properly understood.

"My friend was good and sincere and always helpful but, you know, she could also suddenly fly into a rage if she were jealous."

She still wasn't cheerful when we arrived. She was flitting back and forth from one room to the other, reorganizing the presents without unwrapping them. But then she never did unwrap presents, because then you embarrassed the giver of the gift. She placed an egg beside the yellow rice on the balcony and asked me, "Shall I lay her photo beside the plate? Maybe that's better."

So then we looked in all the closets for the photo album of the vacation before last in Italy, because she was in those pictures with her white poodle and the Morris, but Manda had put everything away for the party, thereby reorganizing a lot of closets and drawers.

Neo fell on his knees, kissed Aunt Yossa's hand with the words, "What a happy chance that the most beautiful lady at the party also happens to be the birthday girl," and asked her to dance.

"In a little while, young man," her mouth said, her eyes were still looking at the closet door behind which lay the right photo album, but her body was already dancing. He whisked her through the room, tossed her up in the air and caught her just above the floor—it must have been a long time since she last soared through the living room because my father had stopped doing it long before, complained of rheumatic pains, a slight hernia, back pain—and she was scared young, her curly gray hair bounced with every toss, and in her eyes each time the fear that bordered on joy. I know this because I used to get tossed by Uncle Didi, my other uncles, my mother's cousins, my Grandpa, my father. They had let me fly while the others lazily lumbered around on the floor.

My aunt flew into her birthday as a girl of one, two, three, four, five years old, and I was paying attention to her eyes in which again and again my own ecstasy was expressed near the ceiling.

Afterward Aunt Manda gave him a compliment. We were leaning against one another, he was tired, panting a little from dancing, the back of his hand against my left thigh for minutes already; more hadn't happened yet, but our fantasies had, in silence, overstepped all bounds a long time ago.

"That you can do that at your age, I mean, how strong you still are." Her clumsy playfulness, no, playful clumsiness, for had she insulted him, she would have done so by means of a nice compliment, because that's how Aunt Manda is; she teases, she flatters, and she laughs at the same time.

While she was pinching those supposed muscles, I read in her eyes the honest disappointment in what was to be found under his shirt. I heard him say, "I've been training a lot with my daughters." Aunt Manda's surprised exclamation, "You have daughters? Oh, how nice. I've only got sons. We tried it five times and then Didi thought enough was enough. How old are your girls? Where is your wife? Why didn't you bring her along?"

A conversation followed. His jokes, her laughter. He had kept trying, too, he said. And perhaps she still wanted a girl, because with him it would succeed the first time, it only took ten minutes, done in a trice, it wasn't a long job. She laughed. He spoke loudly. I didn't listen. The pressure on my thigh disappeared. The hand disappeared. I sought, as if on the run, a quiet little spot in the house, somewhere behind a door, behind the curtain of the foldaway bed, in a *sapulidi* closet, or beside the chest with assorted old paper. I only found faces that wanted to say hello, mouths that wanted to talk or kiss, cheeks that posed for an obligatory peck, hands to shake, moving bodies. I slipped away from my son who pulled me from the hallway into a room to dance.

In the portico there was air. The outside door was shut, no mat jammed under the door like before when there were parties at Grandma's. I looked up the street where it was quiet, cool, too dark, shut the door and took refuge one floor higher, two sets of stairs up, like I used to when I was angry or just wanted to be alone, in front of the door to the upstairs neighbors, who never seemed to be there or were always asleep.

How much later, I don't know, but he found me, in the corner, rolled up like a slug, my eyes red, I suspect, lifted me up onto his lap, put his arms around me, my face against his soft stomach, the hard leather belt with the small buckle pressed painfully into the back of my neck.

I pushed him away. "No," I said, or did I want to say that? "It's wrong, what we're doing. We have to stop this even though it hasn't started yet."

The dark, the hard concrete floor, the prickly doormat. We sought each other's warmth, each other's consolation over the frightening realization that we didn't dare to share with anyone else: being the victim, wanting to be the victim, wanting to belong to the other, to the wrong one.

Have you really forgotten everything, or are you simply too tired to want to put each memory into words? I can understand that. It is, now that I am trying to write down everything that happened as honestly as possible, far easier to remember the moments at which he hurt me, moments at which in retrospect I can later claim he isn't worthy of me, that he isn't as fascinating and special as I thought.

Before Yossa's party, before we had even left the house, I had already really been shocked by him. We were quarrelling, Martin and I, about whether the cockatoo should go or not. He thought not and I thought it should. But it would also be the first time that we would be leaving the bird home alone and all kinds of objections were involved with that.

Neo didn't let us argue for long. He walked into the back yard and in a few minutes had nailed together a door with some wood he had found in our junk shed and some old chicken wire from the neighbors' fence, behind which he imprisoned Kasesa. With bits of wire he braided hinges and fastened the door shut.

"He'll gnaw the wood to pieces," said Martin, as if the improvised door was something to be accepted without question, and Neo replied, "He really won't break it before sun-up."

My grumbling that the bird should be free and that this would be the beginning of the end, wasn't heard. I was dumbfounded, but didn't intervene. If Martin had locked Kasesa up, I would definitely have undone the trelliswork right away, but Neo seemed inviolable.

I'd much prefer to forget them, those moments we had taken

off time and circumstances like our clothing, he and I fifteen or sixteen years old again, in a cramped bathtub: the way we covered each other's backs, chests, scalps with soap, massaged them, rinsed them, lathered them up, massaged, rinsed, until our fingers and toes were pale and wrinkled, the skin seeming to have separated from our bodies so that we could get closer together, our bodies one, the way our thoughts seemed to have been one for such a long time, at least, that's what I believed, that there was no difference anymore between his and my thoughts, our desires were the same, his spirit in me, my spirit in him.

VI

My Kasesa had in no way tried to free itself. It had sharpened its beak on everything except the construction that kept the cage shut.

Neo and I stayed downstairs for a while longer. Martin apologized, he was too tired, he said. He had, in fact, fallen asleep in the back of Neo's car and snored, intermittently, sometimes loudly, then wheezed unsteadily, because he had gotten up very early that morning to get some work done before we left to go to the party. First we had listened to some music, then only to Martin's labored breathing. Neo showed me, after fearfully looking into the rearview mirror and around at Martin, a black-and-blue mark on his neck, right below his shirt collar. "Did I do that?" my eyes had asked. His expression, proud and guilty at the same time, "Yes, you did."

His hand on the short gear shift between us had remained, even though there was no need, and had fondled the knob as if he were feeling up my leg.

Drunk on his scent I tried to breathe him in, through all my pores, through my ears, mouth, nose, my navel, my vagina, through everything that was open I wanted to pull him inside my body. And yet I stood there holding some seeds under Kasesa's beak and didn't move. My nose was very close to his shaggy arm as I heard Martin go upstairs. His fingers clumsy with the wire he had earlier attached with such dexterity. I stroked Kasesa, slowly, my hand through the copper bars.

He tugged at the door. "Do you have a screwdriver?" his voice asked. It was only his voice that spoke.

We heard the bathroom door, the water in the shower, and let the bird be. Like thieves we groped each other's bodies. I was relentless, opened his fly, buried my head in his trousers wet with sweat, the warmth and the scent like a haze around my thinking, with my nose and mouth I sought the opening to his shorts and bit in greedily, hungrily, while he said, "Meisje, think about Martin, Meisje, I. . . oh no. . . ." He was the one who heard the bathroom door again and tensed up, too much silence, and then we threw ourselves contritely and with much excessive talk at the cage, whose latch gave way in a few seconds. Kasesa didn't come out of the cage. The bird seemed to have resigned itself to its own space. Even the next day it stepped out only when coaxed with its favorite food or the hose.

Neo and I played with the bird for a long time, loudly, too audibly for Martin who, under the impression that I would be coming up soon, had left the bedroom door open a crack, and was trying to sleep. Meanwhile, we caressed each other's hands, arms, neck, ears, mouth and nose, and looked into each other's eyes silently until the sun came up and the full moon was still waiting.

"Your Uncle Didi and I got married. It was a big reception with so many people who came from far away. . . . Actually, I

123

was already sick but I had paid it little mind. I thought, maybe you're always supposed to feel ill when you get married. . . I mean. . . because you are the center of attention. But the days that followed I felt the same. A lot of coughing, difficulty breathing, as if somebody were trying to strangle me. My father said to Didi, 'Take her to a doctor.'

"A good doctor, a big sturdy fellow, a Dutch man, but not crude, you know what I mean, a. . . uh. . . a very friendly man. He said nothing. I could see him looking, listening again with that thing, looking again. . . . He called in a lung specialist and then they told my father and Didi the bad news. Myself, I still knew of nothing.

"A hole in my lung as big as a fist. So I was living on only one lung. The doctor had told Didi that it couldn't be treated. I wasn't allowed to do anything anymore, only lie down, stay in bed, like an invalid. Uncle Didi wasn't allowed to sleep with me. We were supposed to pray, he said. Since then, I think, your uncle has become a model believer. He already always went to church on Sunday, but then he started on communion, confession, the whole business, just like my father.

"My mother said to Didi, 'Go to a *doókoon*,' one of those, what do you call them here anyway, somebody with special powers. She thought I had a spell on me, and Yossa also really believes in those kinds of things. They went to the servants to ask if there wasn't a good *doókoon* in the area. In the meantime I was brought to Aunt Fuut's, she was living in Surabaya at that time. I think Didi's mother was afraid I had gotten sick from the cockatoo, so they gave the parrot to Didi's oldest brother who was going to Holland.

"I don't know exactly what happened. All I can say is what I heard from Yossa and your mother later. But I know that it must have been somebody who wanted to take revenge for my marrying Didi. The doctor couldn't believe I had recovered.

He stood there shaking his head over how the hole in my lung had disappeared. A. . . good-looking man, that doctor. I saw him again later in Holland. He had grown old, but. . . um. . . he still looked good, you know. . . though I didn't recognize him because I didn't expect to see him there. Grandpa was laid up in the hospital because of his stomach, and I was there for visiting hours. Suddenly I hear this voice behind me saying something. I won't say what it was, you know what I mean, a person doesn't enjoy hearing those things, I'd prefer it if they said you're friendly, or a good person, at least that does you some good, but so OK, he says something and I don't turn around, of course. Then I feel this hand on my shoulder, and he still knows my name, 'Manda,' he says, 'I never would have thought that I would see you here in such good health.' I told him that I work out every day, play badminton and tennis, and that when there's a party I dance until the band puts their guitars back in their cases, and he had to laugh."

I don't think, Grandma, that I know anybody who is so provocative and prim at the same time. She is perfectly capable of rejecting someone in a way that couldn't be clearer, while the rejection itself only serves to make her more attractive. The manner in which she refuses a compliment demands a bigger compliment, as it were. She fascinates. She captivated me even as a child. I hung on her every word when she told a story. She knows how to turn an all but meaningless incident into a thrilling event. Her expressive eyes and the slight suggestiveness in the combination of the full lower lip with a thin upper lip lends a recurring hint of irony to her prudish way of talking. The unexpected breaks into her stories as if she were trying to veil her words at the last minute, her disarming smile, and in particular the dichotomy between her naive words and the meaningful look in her eyes or the other way around, the child-like innocence on her face together with the naughty text rolling off her tongue, this dichotomy, one she constantly manages to keep in balance as an attitude toward life that has come about naturally, that wasn't acquired—she being too matter-of-fact—typifies my Aunt Manda's unique charm.

Things I was able to keep from Lotte I'd blab to Aunt Manda. When she came through the front door and said hello, she would look into my eyes and discover the things I had been able to keep hidden from the rest of the world.

"Are you in love? Who's the happy man? Is he Indo or Dutch?"

I shook my head. No, of course I wasn't in love. But while washing the dishes she posed the question again. "I can see it in your eyes," she said, "are you in love?" Then I could do nothing but confess.

"Have you already given your first kiss?" she asked two hours after I, fourteen years old, had tasted a French kiss. I wiped my mouth, afraid that the traces could still be see on my lips. I knew for certain that she couldn't have seen me, because we had been alone, just the two of us, in his father's warehouse, a factory shed outside of town, where he practiced with his band, he being the drummer, and from where he had sent the boys home early, locking the shed, because I had come to listen, as promised. When he put his arms around me and my lips were exactly at the level of his chin, because I was standing on my toes, and I smelled his perspiring body, a familiar smell even though I had never felt him this close (every day for over a half year he had waited for me after school on his Puch moped to take me home, me on my bike, and if the wind was in our faces, he would give me a boost by pushing on my back) I wanted to kiss, finally know what it was like: another mouth that sucked onto yours. Outside, the sun bright and painful in my eyes, his saliva still in my mouth as evidence of the summer that had just begun, I thought how lucky it was that I had waited and that he had actually been the first one, because there was nobody else who could have given me my first kiss better. I rode around the industrial terrain a few extra times in order to treasure the long kiss, my tongue still warm and swollen, before I biked home where there would be lots of people celebrating my mother's birthday.

Auntie, the tone of her voice reassuring, a mischievous glimmer in her eye, her mouth hungry for the memory of her first kiss, said, "I can see it in your eyes." Her enthusiasm caused me to tell Aunt Yossa, who was just as eager to hear me tell about such experiences and reacted with equal delight. As scared as I was that my mother would get to know something, I was equally sure that my secret was in good hands with them.

When there were boys roaming around outside the house and I was crawling through the living room on my hands and knees so they wouldn't see me, she asked, "There must be one you like, though?"

I shook my head. "No, none of them is nice enough."

"How about that blond one, then, the one with the red scarf, he has a nice face."

I peered through the bathroom window to see whom she meant and told her, "He's too short."

Then she in turn took another look at the boys who were ringing the doorbell to borrow a bicycle pump, shoving each other recklessly into the front yard, shouting my name and sometimes wrestling with each other, which regularly led to fights.

"Yes, he is small, but if you choose one, then the others will automatically leave you alone. And you have to choose one with whom you can call the shots. Anyhow, a young man keeps growing until he's twenty, and this one's only thirteen or fourteen, I think."

Aunt Divette was surprised they came to see me and not Lotte. While Aunt Manda was pulling the pans and dishes through the suds, Aunt Divette helped me dry them. Lotte had gone to her room with her homework.

"I would never have thought that you would be chased so much by boys. Lotte, I can see, Lotte's always so sociable and talks to everybody, and Lotte looks a lot more like a Dutch girl because of her light skin color and her round eyes. You were always the quiet one. You were shy. That's why you were called Meisje, I think."

"But isn't there that saying about still waters something something?" opted Aunt Manda.

"I always thought you would be more like your mother, she didn't want anything to do with boys. Your father was, I believe, the very first one."

"No, he wasn't," said Aunt Manda, "she did kind of have a boyfriend before Edwin came along. . . a nice lad. . . a Chinese boy. . . rich family. . . he was very. . . um. . . how's that called, for your mother, but at that time she didn't know your father yet, and when Edwin came along, she wanted Edwin instead and so she gave that boy back his ring."

"Sure, but she wasn't like Meisje, causing the boys to come riding around the house every day in such numbers, and anyway Poppa wouldn't have stood for that, boys always had to come inside."

"I don't want them to come in," I said, "I don't think they're nice at all."

"What kind of boys do you think are nice, then?" Aunt Manda asked, full of curiosity.

But as long as Aunt Divette was around she didn't get an answer.

· · ·

There is so much that I don't dare write. I know you hate bragging, and I've already noticed that it sounds arrogant when I honestly try to say what all happened to me. My story isn't believable, but until I started talking about it, I never knew that my experience was an exception, that it isn't the rule that starting at age ten girls are followed around so much by boys, that men suddenly stand in front of you and take off their pants for you. . . . Lotte sometimes didn't even believe me, thought I was making up the things that happened to me between school and home, until she saw with her own eyes what went on, to a far lesser extent, however, simply because of her presence.

Those boys that would wait for me in a big group on the hill near school, she'd already seen. She had to laugh about that. She herself had already made a choice and had asked me if I didn't want to ask Ken, the oldest and biggest of the bunch, if he wouldn't take her to a class dance. Through Lotte I learned to see the advantages of all that attention. All I had to do, in fact, was to choose, Grandma, and it seems like so much fun to be constantly courted and the only thing you have to do is say no in a charming way. . . .

At ten or eleven years old I thought I was very strong. From Grandpa and Aunt Yossa I had learned Indonesian fighting techniques and if the boys in the neighborhood or the boys from school were after me and tried to touch me, I'd toss them on the ground with a leg or a hip throw, sit on top of them and demand that they ask forgiveness, the way we always did when we wrestled on the mattresses in your house until one of the two howled "Sorry, sorry."

When I was first getting to know Martin I liked to wrestle with him, but I was unable to get him down with any throw or movement, and if I did manage in a surprise attack to drag him down onto the floor, it would only be a few seconds before I was lying on the bottom again. He claimed that those boys actually loved having me sit on top of them, that I had no strength to speak of in my arms or legs, and that my fighting technique left a lot to be desired.

With Neo I started wrestling again, and thanks to a little bit of tickling I was able to win, so that wrestling always remained a challenge, and not, as with Martin, merely a put-down.

I was accustomed to bodies around me. The less often we stayed overnight, the more time I spent doing homework in high school, the more I missed the horsing around on the mattresses, the games with my cousins, and I would push my father away whenever he lifted me up to hug me. But the ribbon did pop up again when, among the many boys, I saw the special one who gave me that itchy sensation by his way of looking at me so that all the daily routines became enjoyable again. Sometimes there was nobody for months, but then sometimes there would be a teacher, for instance the old gray-haired history teacher who called me Cleopatra, who would now and then pinch my cheek, or the French teacher, who smelled more masculine than anyone else and whose scent I would take along with me to the following classes. I glowed when he stood beside me, slightly leaning over me, to point out a phrase or word in my translation with a yellow nicotine-stained finger, mumbling something, and I, in a fog because of his presence, would turn crimson, nodding, not listening to what he was telling me.

In the summertime, but sometimes also in the spring and autumn, there were many boys I dreamed beside me, his head on my pillow, his leg flopped over mine, his breath in my neck, not more, only that extra warmth, because Lotte had her own bed by now, so I slept alone.

I wasn't looking for anything besides that hot warmth. At night often my little brother would crawl in bed with me because he was scared of the dark and he had a room to himself.

That was fine, too, his head against my back, his small leg over my thighs.

Of course there was a difference. I have to be honest. Being with my little brother, was warm, cozy, nice, as well as a drag because he would pull all the sheets off, or it would get too hot in bed, we'd start to sweat, and he would lie there fast asleep and I would lie awake.

I longed for the warmth in my head, the tingling through my whole body just by laying eyes on that one boy biking past my house, a glimpse of him at the baker's, suddenly his scent, his shuffling, his voice behind me at the check-out counter, and yet that one boy would the next day, or even that same afternoon, be another already, as long as there was that tingling that I tried to bring back at night, the sheet pulled over my head while I imagined him lying on top of me, his body heavy, or only that he was looking at me with eyes that see me from head to toe.

In my room, Lotte nowhere near, I showed Aunt Manda my diary, in the back of which I'd written the names of the boys that gave me that special feeling, that trembling inside, the ribbon.

We enjoyed the same things, Aunt Manda and I, my boys became her boys, her past became mine, but one day I lost the innocence that even now still makes Aunt Manda sparkle. She remained fourteen. When Didi asked her to marry him he was actually offering to be her father alongside grandfather Hermanus, so she remained a child, uninhibited, with that disarming smile that tames everything, but also with that longing under her skin.

You didn't flirt, Grandma, you didn't even look. You had learned to give every man, especially the men you thought

131

were worth looking at, the cold shoulder. "Your Grandpa is very jealous," you explained to us whenever pots and plates went flying through the flat and you locked yourself in Aunt Yossa's room, Grandpa pleading in a soft voice, "Sorry, Lotte, I apologize, come on, open the door." Even on your honeymoon he wanted to murder some man because there had been too much infatuation in his eyes when he greeted you. "I'll never dance more than two dances with one and the same man," you said, "otherwise your Grandpa gets difficult."

But there were plenty of men to keep you dancing all night. Lotte didn't think this was fair, "Why does Grandpa keep dancing with Aunt Leonie, then?" (That Dutch woman with the full pale breasts that came into view when she leaned over towards Aunt Yossa, who was married to Grandma's youngest brother for five years, but then divorced him over four years ago, even though after the divorce she had had two children who looked an awful lot like him; who still came to all the family get-togethers anyway because she couldn't bear to miss them, and asked Grandfather Hermanus and my father to dance time and time again while refusing the other men politely.)

"Grandpa is a man," said Grandma, "that's why. . . ."

What I wonder is whether Aunt Manda only knows the ribbon the way it runs through your body when you feel the admiring looks, the hungry eyes that finger your skin, the smile that responds to yours as fully, but still doesn't know what it's like when your skin begins to tingle because of an unshaven jaw wildly skidding over your breasts, the hand that hunts and rests between your legs, hunts again and teases and hunts and rubs until you don't know anymore that there's a body behind which you hide yourself.

. . .

Martin was different, the first young man who talked while he danced, who didn't pull my body close to him, but held his hand lightly on my shoulder, who didn't pay me any compliments, but who shouted his daydreams into my ear above the sound of Santana and Pink Floyd: the trips he was going to take, the enthralling cultures he was going to experience, the research he was going to undertake some day somewhere on one of the Indonesian islands, because that's where I came from, after all, that country, but from which island though, exactly? Regardless of whether the rhythm was slow or fast, he would hop from one foot to the other, move his right hand a lot while talking, and not notice that it was tiring for me to try and catch his words above the volume of the speakers that elevated the high school assembly hall to a dance hall.

"I was born here," I shouted back in his ear.

"But your parents, then, from which island do they come?"

"Don't know," I confessed.

He hollered his question over and over into my ear, and each time I shouted back, "I don't know."

"You really don't know where your parents were born?" The music had fallen silent. He looked into my eyes seriously shocked.

I searched, was there a name I had heard dropped often, a name that seemed like that of a city or an island? In his eyes I saw the censure, the expression I loathed: So, are you really that stupid?

How could I prove that I wasn't stupid, but that I hadn't wanted to know anything about my parents' past, because being different was already such a burden that I didn't also want to remember what made me different from the rest.

"Batavia?" (My answer was a question.)

"Aha, Java," he said, "that's the exotic island at the top of my list. Let's go there together."

133

. . .

I love the heat, the burning pain at the level of my chest that is caused by desire, the not yet stilled hunger for his hand in my hand, his mouth on my mouth, his thighs around mine.

Martin was the first one to take away my illusions about fulfilled desire. Actually, as I now know, I prefer the reveling in desire to the moment at which that desire is fulfilled.

Already in the beginning he upset the line between reality and fantasy, the border I cherished. Under the blankets, all alone in the dark, I let everything happen and I'd pull the strings so that my characters danced the way it suited me. But he spoke my dreams out loud, called travel agencies, sent my short stories to publishers. His word was the first step toward the deed. He and I, traveling together, a big trip, he and I, writing together. He, as an anthropology student, wanted to write about other cultures. I, who liked nothing better than to nestle into my dreams, saw myself on a practically uninhabited island under a palm tree chewing on a ball-point, being a writer, but would, without his booking tickets with the cheapest airline—paid for out of his savings—never have known that there are mosquitoes flying around in paradise.

Aunt Manda and Uncle Didi's living room was crowded. Men and women talked in hushed voices. The cold from outside still hung in the room. Maybe I still had my coat on, unbuttoned, and on my lap the hungry child—the rissoles and the *lumpias* had just been put in the oven—who was scared to walk around because of Uncle Didi's giant dragonlike reptile beside the coffee table, of which, as a child, I had also been afraid. Like a police officer my mother was concerned about keeping the living room door shut because at the arrival of each guest an icy draft would come in as well. I can't remember the circumstances exactly anymore. It was as if we were waiting for something. Maybe not all the guests had arrived, maybe there weren't enough parking spaces on the street, and that for a moment in-laws and acquaintances were saddled up with one another without a common denominator. I can see Grandma, with her coat on also because the heater compensated too slowly, and I can see Aunt Yossa setting out coasters on the coffee table and the end tables. She shuffles among the guests, holds them by a knee, and everybody seems to follow her movements, waiting for a common topic of conversation. There had been a funeral, I thought, no, Martin was walking around with his camera; there had been a wedding, Aunt Manda's youngest son had gotten married after a year ago divorcing a woman he'd married six months earlier. His new wife was pregnant and already close to term. The bride and groom were photographed in the back yard in front of the aviary because that was the only place that Martin, as the wedding-photographer, felt was appropriate for color photos.

She was beaming, Aunt Manda, when she came into the living room with coffee, and looked younger than the bride. "You must all be parched by now, I'm sure." She set the large tray full of mugs down on the coffee table, and suddenly the company realized that it was a party.

"What a lovely figure you have!" exclaimed the Dutch lady, sister of the bride, herself a little heavy around the hips, two-thirds of her full breasts showing above her low-cut neckline making her little round belly quickly forgotten at the waist. Aunt Manda, apologetically blushing slightly, as if the lady had caught her stealing, magically produced her mischievous smile, ran her hands awkwardly over her hips and flat stomach, and said, in a whisper, yet audible enough for the entire company that looked up at her and gobbled up her girlish motions, "No, not at all, I've gotten heavier! Did you know that for the first time in my life I'm a size eight. I really haven't been exercising enough because of the bad weather. . . ." Her hands flit over her breasts, then her fingers turned the collar of her high V-neck dress inside out, causing one of her bra straps to show, and pulled out a piece of white foam rubber. "See, it's all fake," she said triumphantly.

Neo asked me to travel with him. He saw the photos that Martin and I had taken during our many wanderings in various parts of the world, whispered, "I am jealous about that, that Martin has a wife like you who thinks things like that are fun and who goes with him," flipped through Martin's black-and-white repros in professional journals, read his photographic stories in chic magazines, and said, staring at the photo of a thirteen-year-old girl wearing nothing but a grass skirt, "Haven't you two ever been to the Trobriand Islands?"

"I wanted to see them most, but when I met Meisje I focused more on the Indonesian islands, and in all the years since then for one reason or another it just never happened."

"What would you two think of all of us going there together sometime?"

Martin was enthusiastic, made inquiries as to how we could get there, made an itinerary and ferreted out exactly which flights on which days of the week and from which ports which ships would get us to the islands. I knew already, though, Grandma, that Neo would organize it in such a way that Martin wouldn't come along on this trip. We had never mentioned out loud that we were both dying for some time just the two of us could be alone together, but every sigh, the tiniest movement of his hand, every look betrayed our longing.

Martin himself said after a few days of preparation, "Actually we can't afford to take that trip. I have to polish off my dissertation first. If I go on a trip during the coming months then it will be to go to Kalimantan to finish up the last phase of my research. We'll have to put it off."

Neo said nothing more about it, but a few days later he showed up at the door, a broad smile on his face, in his hand a big silk-screen of two cockatoos, one plucked bald but with a full crest, the other still in all its glory, who were nuzzling each other.

"I have a brilliant proposal to make," he said. "What would you two think of my paying for Meisje's trip to the Trobriand Islands, and also his trip," he was pointing at the silk-screen with the delicate pastel tints, "so that they can let themselves be inspired to a brilliant coproduction. Your cockatoo, Meisje, originally came from this area, and it seems to me it would be a fantastic project to take the cockatoo back there and see how the animal reacts to its country of origin. I'm convinced that you're going to write the most beautiful poems of your life there."

It was too transparent, Grandma, I thought Martin was going to kick Neo out of the house, but he said, "A fantastic plan."

Neo laid a hand on his shoulder and continued, "And you can come to the islands of love after you've finished your research in Borneo, then the four of us can still travel around a bit together."

After all these years I still don't know when Martin means something or not. The same evening that I saw Martin again at the school reunion after all those years, and we danced together the whole evening, he deflowered me. He hadn't been my first boyfriend, but he was the first one I allowed between my legs. Precisely because of his indifference, precisely because he somehow showed in words but not in other ways that he was in love with me, I seemed to want physical proof. I wouldn't let him go, literally hung on his neck, buried my head in his armpit.

He brought me home in his old swaying Citroên, but when he drove right up in front of the house, I told him to drive farther. At this, he obediently stepped on the accelerator and stopped the ugly duck, as the Dutch call it, fifteen feet down the street. "No, farther," I said, and he stopped another thirty feet farther on.

"No, drive out the end of the street and turn the corner."

"Don't you live here?"

"Keep driving," I commanded.

There, I started kissing him, kisses he eagerly responded to, because earlier, in the hallway of the school and next to the car in the parking lot, we had also kissed. Then his hand had immediately, during the first French kiss, slid between my legs and I had spontaneously pushed his hand away. But now I myself laid his hand on my breasts, and ran my lips over his body.

"We're right in the street," he said. "Let me find a little spot in the woods first."

While he drove off in search of a path in the woods and an open dark spot among a lot of trees far away from the high-rise apartments, I loosened his belt, breathed in the scent of his body, drew his warm, slightly damp, crumpled member out of his tight white briefs and let it grow in my hands and mouth.

His hands gripped my head and pulled me away from his lap. The car was standing still and he had turned off the engine. He tried to get up, felt around in his pockets, and pulled a little packet out of his back pocket. I didn't get why he had suddenly put a halt to our love-making and why he was now fiddling with a bit of paper. Did he want to chew gum at a moment like this?

Suddenly I felt the chill of the night, heard the sounds of the woods, saw the condensation on the windows, smelled the damp woods, felt the rough texture of the broken seat, got scared that somebody was spying, and was annoyed at the squeaking of the rocking car.

He had put the condom on, cursing because it didn't want to go on right, and while he was messing with it I understood what its purpose was. So that's what that looks like, I thought, and now I'm going to get fucked.

VII

"My girls don't do things like that."

My mother's steadfast faith in her daughters obliged me to live according to her rules, and without realizing it I fought stubbornly against her confident voice in my head. Every time it was getting to be fun somewhere and I got the urge to throw my head back, feel the back of the chair and forget about everything except the moment itself, something would start gnawing at me, a Jiminy Cricket who wandered through my body tapping my profligate muscles here and there with his cane and sternly calling back to order every muscle that was just about to relax. At some point during puberty I caught on to just how often my mother's cricket spoiled the fun. The creature was too late when I abandoned myself to my first kiss, and after that there was no turning back. I'm not sure, but my first real love might well have started with my first real kiss. You were fond of him, Grandma, and Aunt Yossa and Aunt Manda always inquired about Peter with the green eyes. You all only met him about three times, but still, years afterward, Aunt Manda asked "How's Peter? A very appealing boy he was."

It was impossible for the cricket to come between us with his cane. My eyes were shut and there was nothing but the embrace. By his light stroking of my breasts I knew that breasts were growing there, and without moving, like a dream that could go on forever, I let him have his way. My abandon was eternity. This was what is called heaven, I thought, and I hoped never to wake up. I succumbed. My hands did nothing, my mouth, my body received his tender caring love. That was all, and so he discovered, without hurting me, that he was too old, and I too young, and no words were needed to maintain the limits. He found an older girlfriend and came to wrestle with me now and then, provoked me, and now, twenty-six years after the fact, I think maybe I provoked him too. My defense was temptation. He tried to kiss me, but it was over, I couldn't do that anymore, and we rolled in the grass, whereby I thought it fun that he was stronger, the way he sat on me, my back on the ground, his crotch lightly on my stomach, his hands holding my wrists lovingly not roughly against the damp earth, his face with the greedy mouth above my face, and I turned my head every which way to escape from the kiss that I still really wanted to taste again, but which I forbade myself out of pride. I won longing. After that there was no kiss anymore except his. I didn't want to kiss anymore so as not to forget how good a kiss can be. I don't know whether it was because of my mother that I didn't cry when it was over. She had informed us about the conditions of love, "The man must be older, bigger, more intelligent, richer, so that as a woman you can lean on him, not the other way around, because then everything will go wrong."

Peter wasn't very much bigger than I, his education wasn't the same as mine, he didn't want to continue in higher education, started working as a photographer's assistant, stood behind the counter, made black-and-white shots for passports, wanted to play drums for his own enjoyment, he said, because as a musician you couldn't get rich and even though he was older, I could get the better of him with words. Because of me he read the paper, because of me he went to museums, I gave him Dylan Thomas' *Under Milkwood* for his birthday, he read James Bond aloud to me.

The young men after him I only kissed in my imagination. They received his eyes, his mouth, his lips, his scent, his hands, his disarming smile.

I would like to see him, no, not see, feel him again, to know whether my memory perfected him or whether he was really the most tender one. In fact, everything was already over before he carefully told me that there was another girl, a blonde, who wore lots of eyeliner, who went to bed with him, a woman really, already nineteen, a year older than he was, who took the pill and with whom he had gone into the woods after the party to which he had invited me, but to which I hadn't gone so as not to risk an argument with my mother. It had been too bad, he said, because he liked me more, but that fourteen was, unfortunately, too young to be having sex.

My cousins said, "Never throw out an old coat until you've found a new one." That's why I was prepared for when Peter would tell me one day that I didn't fit him anymore. And I, too, had made sure to have extra coats, boys I thought were nice, of all ages, who also stopped by the house when I wasn't home and talked with my mother, with my father, or with Lotte. Before me he had had a girl who was so beautiful that I couldn't stop looking at her, because it was as if she weren't real, her face, her mouth, her eyes, her legs, but also the way she walked, the way she put tomatoes in a brown paper bag and the way she wrote the price on the bag afterward. She worked at the green grocer's on Saturdays, and on the national celebration of the queen's birthday she had had to kiss the champion cyclist, a sweaty suntanned man who gave Lotte and me the creeps because we thought he was old and ugly, and smiling at the photographer from the local paper she had placed a laurel wreath around the cyclist's neck.

Because he had left her, the prettiest girl I had ever seen, much older than I, almost a woman to me, I knew our relationship would also come to an end.

They said she was jealous of me, that she had cried for days, and that her mother had told Peter's father that she wanted to commit suicide when she found out that he was escorting me home from school on his Puch every day while she was still his girl. I had seen her on the bus with her girl friend. The girl friend had been humming the Dutch golden oldie "Peter, Peter, Peter, Can't You See, That I'm Just So Unhappy," when Lotte and I got on the bus and bought a ticket from the driver. We were all on our way to the same party, where he was supposed to be waiting for me, and she pulled a compact mirror out of her purse, touched up her lips, dabbed powder on her nose and fussed over a pimple on her forehead. Her girl friend said, "Oh quit it, stop looking at that mirror all the time; you know, the longer you look the bigger it gets."

I had no purse, no mirror, had never made myself up, and looked at my reflection in the bus window. Did I have pimples? I had never paid any attention before and didn't know it was a bad thing, one of those red spots on your face, worried that if I had them he would want to exchange me for another that evening, and knew for certain that everything was temporary, even that which seemed to last forever.

Maybe I was fourteen, maybe I was older already, when Aunt Manda told me that I had to remain pure for the only true man with whom I wanted to live. I had just started menstruating and my mother had told every member of the family, who all came to congratulate me, "What did I hear, Meisje, you've already become a woman!"

She didn't live in the little apartment above the barbershop anymore, but had moved to a newly built-up neighborhood outside of Amsterdam. We were both standing in the kitchen spreading salmon salad on little pieces of toast. Several hours before, Uncle Didi had chased off a group of boys, friends of my cousins', who had stopped by the house and been revving up their motorbikes leaning on the throttle. "All those filthy bikes are going to kill my birds," he had shouted as he ran out into the street in his old brown slippers, waving his fist, shaking with rage. "Get the hell out of here. You bums can't possibly be thinking my nieces would want to hang around with the likes of you. Get out of here before I beat the living daylights out of you. Long-haired cheeseheads, who the hell do you think you are?!" It had been convincing, and I, embarrassed, had gone on the pretext of mailing a letter to tell them that my uncle might say all he wanted to, but that I thought they were cool, and that I'd sneak out that night together with Lotte, maybe with our cousins, too, to talk with them, and maybe go out dancing somewhere. But when I saw them all standing there on the street corner, they suddenly stopped talking, and all eyes turned to me, so I quickly looked at the ground and walked the other way, my hands deep in my pockets.

"Uncle Didi explained to me that men have to have a lot of experience, or else they won't know how to make it pleasurable for a woman, but a woman has to be a virgin, because it feels tight inside, and that's pleasant for a man, that he's the first one to push through that little membrane. After the Second World War Uncle Didi practiced an awful lot with Australian girls because otherwise he wouldn't have known how to do it with me."

(My mother, too, had warned me that I shouldn't be easy,

that they say Indies girls are hot and willing, and that you have to watch out because of that, men will chase you because they're hoping they can use you. But my Indies girl friends and I were called the prudish toads at school, because the Dutch girls of our age, all very curious, had already tried what felt good and what didn't.

"You have to enter marriage as a virgin," my mother had said, "especially because you're Indies it's so important that you remain a virgin. A man, when he marries, wants to be the first one."

"And men, then?" Lotte and I were always looking for what was and wasn't fair. We helped do the dishes while our cousins ran outside right after the meal to go play ball. "That isn't fair," we cried, and then my mother would get our cousins back inside. They were each handed a dish towel, complained, let a dish or mug fall on purpose, but stayed in the kitchen until all the dishes had been done.

"With men it's different. Your father did it for the first time on our wedding night, but Uncle Didi does have more experience which I do think is better, because Aunt Manda enjoys sexual relations and I don't, really.")

"Isn't it a pity for those Australian girls that they aren't tight inside anymore?" I dared to ask Aunt Manda a lot, like whether Uncle Didi knew that she wore foam pads in her bra, whether that bothered him, whether menstruation was painful, how much blood came out, if the blood was poisonous, whether she used tampons and whether it was painful to bear a child, questions I didn't pose my mother.

"Uncle Didi says that there are girls who make themselves available for this and that those girls don't want to marry. Those girls are girls of pleasure."

. . .

145

Actually I've never been unfaithful to Martin.

He took me to Indonesia and on Bali, when he and two fellow students threw themselves into researching religion and fertility, I would saunter, bored, down the beach and receive attentions from Fernando, the beautiful Brazilian, son of a rich industrialist, who had started wandering because he and his father had fought. Martin and I had been looking for months already for ways, as he solemnly put it, to satisfy me sexually. I was beginning to understand what he meant, when he kept asking, "Did you come? Did you come?" The many books he had acquired for me on the subject and had opened to the right pages made me suspect that he meant the volcanic eruptions in my dream from which I awoke blushing, a slight feeling of guilt at having been happy in my sleep with somebody other than Martin, with whom I lived.

He had tried to reach his goal with his tongue, his hand, and with other body parts by friction, by bumping, by pushing, and for nights at a stretch we had endlessly, like gymnasts, tried out all the positions and games until we fell asleep, dead tired, without any results, one on either side of the bed. He didn't want any orgasms himself anymore, he had said, until I, too, reached a high point, and no matter how I tried to convince him, he wasn't to be mollified. We had totally lost track, during our struggle to get me to climax, of the ribbon.

Because of Fernando, who came and lay down next to me on the beach in his bikini suit and blew into my ear while I gazed at the wild waves, the ribbon came back. I crawled in the sand, rubbed my stomach and breasts with the wet grains, hid my body beneath a thick layer that I patted flat, a damp patty on my skin in which I drew little figures, let the waves wash over my legs and my back, lay my head in the sand, grains in the corners of my eyes and ears, and became sea. After feeling the sun on my skin for days, he made an attempt to cover me in a sarcophagus of sand. I let him do as he pleased, had already covered my feet and calves with sand myself while talking about the pyramids, because he'd been there and he'd read a lot about them. I sighed, lay back, and shut my eyes. He worked quickly, had me all covered up, and only my face was still free. Then he drew tiny little flowers and big tigers, dragons and snakes, women's and men's bodies lovingly in the carefully flattened sand, told me in his funny English about what he was drawing and made up stories about his drawings. I was the woman he had loved in another lifetime, he said, she had died and all her property would be buried with her. "We will live together forever in the death," he said. Because of the teasingly slow outlining movement of his index finger in the sand that separated my upper thigh from his hand, I suddenly realized what Martin and I had sought in vain. I didn't slap the sand off my body when I followed him.

It was only to see whether it would happen with him. I did it for Martin, to remember how it was when we still caressed out of curiosity and longing. Fernando wildly tore the batik beach wrap and my bikini bottom off my body before the wooden door had blown shut behind us. He whispered to me in Portuguese words that should have aroused me, but suddenly I felt the itch of the sand on my back and in my hair, and while he went up and down above me, panting, and sweat spattered from his forehead onto my face and breasts, I peered at the bamboo walls and the ceiling and counted the lizards that were meanwhile idly snapping at mosquitoes.

That time with Fernando I told Martin about right away. He was back early from the villages, the two students were reading out on the porch and I ran unwashed, dirty from the beach and the strange sweat, into the Balinese yard as he was just stepping out of the communal bathroom, white towel around his waist. I stammered something, pulled him along to our room, a small stuffy whitewashed space with two narrow beds that Martin had pushed together straightaway upon our arrival and explained to him that I had hoped for an orgasm, so I'd know what it was supposed to be like, that I was sorry, that I felt dirty, shabby because it had been wrong and he took me in his arms, kissed my face, my ears, my neck, my arms, underarms and slid his lips all over my body, sought out every nook and cranny, and that time it happened, that night after we had forgotten for hours where we were, the sheets covered with sand and I cleaned by his saliva, everything from that whole afternoon ebbed away. For the first time I became storm.

Neo said, "It isn't because you're so beautiful that I had to get to know you at all costs. Nor because your skin is such a gorgeous brown, even though I love your shiny skin and would like nothing more than to caress it. Nor because you write pretty good books or because, just like me, you like cockatoos. Nor because for your age you still have such a young body and such a girlish way of walking. Beautiful women I have seen often enough, much more beautiful than you, not to hurt your feelings, and from when I was nineteen up until the day I got to know you, married or not, for money or not, I used to sample one or two a week like a rutting bear, with the exception of the dry periods when I was on vacation with my wife. After an hour, sometimes after a night, and as an exception, after two nights, I quickly ran back to my wife and children. But what fascinates me about you is something else. It's as if there's a very small bright light hidden inside you that starts shining out through your eyes and your mouth onto your surroundings as soon as you start talking, and I keep wanting to be in your light."

. . .

After Fernando the idea of kissing another, or feeling another's hands move over my back or stomach was scary to me. Martin liked nothing better than to pleasure me until I begged him, "Stop, oh, stop I can't take any more." If I look back now, Grandma, I think I was happy then, but in my diary from that time I read pensive poems suggesting disappointment with what the benefits of becoming an adult are. I seem to be nostalgic for my childhood, fantasize about being a twelve-year-old, relive the innocent wrestling games on the goat field in the woods behind my parents' street where, on long summer days, the whole family would have a picnic, play tag and hide-and-seek, where I was a Wild West Indian on Grandpa's back as he crawled through the tall grass, rearing up now and then so I'd fall off his back, and then tickling me until I cried "I give up," where the uncles would throw me and my cousins, all the girls and boys, high into the air as if we were balls. "You weigh nothing," said Uncle Didi. "You're light as a feather, hold tight or else the wind might carry you off to the North Pole and then you'll be a little brown polar bear with green icicles hanging off your pug nose."

I also had headaches, stomach aches, slept badly and wasn't interested in doing anything. Instead of studying, I wrote fairy tales and poems. It aggravated Martin to see my textbook open to the same page three days running. It always smelled musty in our little room where we shared a full-sized bed, and which contained two desks and two chairs, with no more space for furniture. If I brought a girl friend home he thought she was stupid, ugly or childish. If I brought a male friend home he'd say, "He only wants to go to bed with you."

And yet, I think, I was still possibly even very happy. . . .

Martin thought it was too early to have a baby. He was

planning another trip to Bali for another research project, a follow-up on the previous one, and wasn't ready to share me with a baby, he said. I could feel our son, already talked to him, walked on the beach with him and collected sea shells.

"We're going to get married," I phoned my mother, "because you're going to be a grandmother."

"Didn't I know it." She sounded proud. "Recently I dreamed my dead brother came to ask me for some rice. At that point I was already thinking of you. You're going to have a son!"

(That's also how it went with Aunt Manda when she had been pregnant with her third boy. Aunt Yossa had dreamed that an old Javanese man, the hairs of his *sik* gray, came asking for rice. When the boy was born Aunt Manda called him Jesse because that was a good name for a girl, too. She let the boy's hair grow well below his shoulders and every day or two she'd put curlers in it. Uncle Didi, returning from a long naval voyage, was furious when he saw Jesse, left his bag in the middle of the small living room and ran downstairs with the boy where, after pounding loudly on the landlord, the barber's, door even though it was Sunday, he demanded that the long black ringlets be chopped off at the scalp.)

About what happened after we moved, after the baby was born, really, I'd rather not write. Martin and I had been doing carpentry work and painting day in day out. We had made a livable apartment from a dump. I thought it was scary, such a big house. One room to cook and eat in, with a shower stall between the toilet and the stove, and upstairs a big room that we had divided into two. One for the baby, a handmade twin bed with a desk on either side. Suddenly there was all this storage space. Our handmade bookshelves were still so empty, and the clothes closet was too roomy for what little clothing we had. We still hadn't gotten used to locking not only a front door, but a back door as well, and there was a break-in. Our closets and desks had been turned inside out, our LPs and our stereo had been stolen. The ring my father had given me at our efficient wedding ceremony, along with three other couples in twenty minutes on a Tuesday morning at the city hall, had also been taken by the indifferent thief, who had gone and left Martin's expensive camera lying on his desk. Martin asked me to look through his desk drawers while he went to have lunch with the editor-in-chief of a paper because the latter wanted to take him on as a staff reporter, to see whether his father's signet ring, inherited from his grandfather, great-grandfather, and so forth, might also had been stolen. I went through one drawer after another with a fine-tooth comb, and in the bottom one, the deepest one, I found a shoe box, its lid clamped tightly to the somewhat torn box with a rubber band, in which he kept his letters.

I shouldn't have read them, actually I shouldn't even have removed the rubber band, and left the lid the way it was. The postmark on the topmost envelope I noticed was a date when we already knew each other. To know for sure, I opened the envelope to see when the letter had been dated, but got distracted by the opening words, which were more intimate than I had ever dared to use with Martin, and when I went through the stack, at first only in search of dates, of legible postmarks, I found letters from the same person sent to general delivery, Bali, during our first long trip, and I started reading, Grandma, which was stupid, because after those letters it was never the same again.

My mother should have been my model. But she is much too perfect, so I couldn't identify with her.

"I wanted to be a pediatrician, or a surgeon in cardiology.

The headmistress of the high school, Sister Ignatius, had told me that I had the brains for it. My father had always hoped that my brother Johan would go to university, and after his death I wanted at least one of the children to have a diploma to be proud of. But I fell in love with your father. He looked so masculine in his uniform. And his eyes. . . . A real lady's man. He had his brother-in-law deliver love letters they had both labored over for hours to our house. Your father had the imagination and was full of romantic notions, his brother-in-law had gone to high school and was better at Dutch, so they wrote the most beautiful poems together. Your father helped me with math, he had the insight even though he hadn't had any schooling, and he wrote my essays for me, which I then corrected so that they were written in faultless Dutch. That's how I got good grades, because the talent to make things up you inherited from him. Your father is more creative and intelligent than I am, but he had the misfortune that his father died young and that he was therefore never encouraged to learn. I didn't want to outdo him, that isn't good, that as a woman you have more diplomas than your husband.

"Just look at Aunt Divette, she finished high school and it went to her head. She preferred Dutch men, while Indo boys with a very good job were turning circles around her. But as an Indies girl you didn't get a Dutch man with a high school diploma, that's why she married somebody who hadn't finished vocational training the first time, and the second time she made the same mistake with an Amsterdammer who presented himself as a car mechanic, but who in fact only pumped gas. My father even warned her, 'First go with him to where he works and take a look at that garage he claims to own,' because he couldn't imagine that this guy with his lame stories could be running his own business.

"I told her too, 'Once you're married with him, you'll have

to accept that he is what he is. There's nothing you can do about it.' But when she's angry, she keeps harping on how he lied to her. A man like that is bound to start drinking, especially if he grew up drinking beer, and then the marriage is bound to fail.

"My youngest sister, Eva, only did a domestic science degree here in Holland, and she managed it because it didn't make her feel as if she were too good for that farmer's son from Groningen who asked her to marry him. And look at how well she's doing now in Australia. My father said, 'Use your common sense. Look at Divette, why do you have to go for a Dutch man, too?' But that fellow was trustworthy, even though she happened to meet him at a bus stop, of all places. She couldn't tell your Grandpa that, naturally, as I'm sure you can understand, because we weren't supposed to take home boys we'd met on the street.

"In financial terms, Eva has it better than any of us, but you can also see in each photo they send us that that unassuming man truly loves her and thinks the world of her. He is always ready to give her a plane ticket to see her parents if she's homesick, and he flies his in-laws over regularly.

"There is nothing wrong with a mixed marriage. That kind of marriage has just as many chances of going on the rocks as a marriage between Indos, but you shouldn't want to be better in everything than your husband, because then you'll lose your respect for him, and he will feel inferior."

Actually, actually I've never really been unfaithful to Martin.

Michiel I wouldn't ever have kissed, if Martin hadn't refused to talk about those letters. The lines from the letters that offered tidy proof of nocturnal meetings with a nurse when he and I weren't living together yet, but long after he had bound himself to me in words, he brushed off with, "I'm not responsible for what *she* writes." He denied everything, threw the box of letters out the bedroom window into the little back yard, poured gasoline all over them and set them on fire. Afterward he wanted to hear nothing more about it, ever, while each night, when we were lying in bed side-by-side, I would start up again about the letters.

Martin refused the job offer, but let himself be sent to all manner of places around the world to be able to write about existing problems from a historical and cultural perspective, and since he was entirely wrapped up in his work and studies, there was still some time left now and then for the baby, but not for me.

Michiel biked with me and the baby through the woods, helped with grocery shopping, listened with me to classical music he had taped for me, repaired our washing machine and refrigerator, and was shocked when I told him Martin and I hadn't made love in several months, hadn't even kissed.

With Michiel I found consolation. One day I noticed I was starting to feel the ribbon when he sat beside me, hoping that he would put his hand on my knee while we were talking, so then I tried to talk to Martin again.

"We shouldn't get in each other's way," said Martin, "I'm happy you aren't a saint, either." Two days later I was sick and Martin wouldn't be home for another three days because of a conference, so Michiel and I crawled under the blankets. He was sweet, considerate, and treated me like a queen, but when I came, which happened easily, I cried over Martin.

Thanks to Michiel, Martin was able to take all those little trips, write all those articles, make a name for himself as a travel writer. I honestly wouldn't have done it, Grandma, if Martin had objected, but Martin said himself, "We shouldn't forbid each other to have those experiences." And when I asked him if maybe he had some girlfriend somewhere, he said, "Do you think I'd have time for that if I already never get to see you and the boy?"

Michiel and I were taking the same courses and seminars, and he had persuaded me to register for the course through which I got to know David. The blackboard beside the little departmental office was full of course sections and seminar groups. I was glad that Michiel chose for me, because all those terms on the board were meaningless to me, Grandma, I stared at it like I would at a menu with French dishes when I only want to eat *soto ayam*.

Sexual Preferences
Sexual Therapy
Sexuality and Role Models
Sexuality and Power
Sadomasochism
Pedophilia
Self-Gratification and Women
Sexuality and Violence
Sexual History
Sexuality and the Elderly
Sexuality and Pregnancy
Sexual Apathy Among Women
Sexual Urges and Upbringing
Sex Education
Exhibitionism Among Women
Exhibitionism Among Men
Children and Sexuality
Sexuality and Animals
Sexuality and Legislation
Sexual Behavior Among Inmates
Unwelcome Intimacies

David, a full professor, was teaching the course Sexuality and Power. During our first encounter, when I went to his office to register for the course, my child in tow, he said, "Do you think you can handle that, a difficult course alongside the responsibility of caring for a child?"

"Martin, my husband, also cares for him," I said timidly, because he had been the first instructor who had shown concern about my being a mother.

"It's a difficult course which will demand a lot of you mentally and physically. You will be expected to test your own limits. That requires a lot of time, and you'll get up and go to bed with everything that goes on in the course."

"That's OK. Martin feels I should take all the courses I think are important to take, too, even though that will demand a lot of energy."

"Why do you need permission from this Martin, your friend or husband, which is he again?"

"I don't, I'm just saying he stands behind me."

"Why do you bring him up when we're talking about you?"

And when I got angry, he said, "Wouldn't you agree that you're overreacting a little? Are you trying to convince yourself, perhaps?"

He made me nervous. During the course he'd sit down next to me, even when there wasn't an empty seat. He would pull up a chair and place it between me and whomever was sitting next to me, saying, "Excuse me." The others always made room for him. I could smell his after-shave. He also used a deodorant, always wore a plaid flannel shirt, and had pale hands, delicate fingers, didn't wear a watch although he would set a little clock in front of himself on his desk and play with it now and again, only when speaking, not when he wasn't talking or listening. He was the only instructor without a beard.

Already during the first break he stood next to me, "I'm

having a party tonight with a few other professors. Are you coming?"

I shook my head, no, said nothing, but kept standing there. I think I spilled my coffee or burned my fingers on the hot plastic cup, so the coffee in any event landed on the floor.

Some days later he leaned against the vending machine while I waited on the thin stream that was slowly filling my cup, and he leaned toward me and whispered in my ear, "When a sexual tension builds up between people, as it's building up between us, then they have to pay attention to that attraction or else they will accumulate enormous amounts of frustration, and people who are frustrated aren't fit psychologists."

"Did you ever consider that I might want to use the knowledge I gain here in another way than as a psychologist?"

"As long as you have so little familiarity with your own feelings that you can't perceive what's going on between us as an important emotion, then you've learned nothing here."

That was David, Grandma, that tall, slightly older, but very attractive man—at the time I thought he was old, but maybe he was only ten years older than I was—I brought over to your house once, because he was interested in my background. He held the door for you, Grandma, and Aunt Yossa thought he was gallant. Due to his questions you told a story I hadn't heard before.

"There is a boy, maybe I was twelve, maybe eleven, I can't remember, naturally, and he was interested in me, I think, because he keeps walking by when I'm feeding the chickens for my father and mother, sweeping the front porch, or doing other chores my parents told me to do. He says hello, and a short while later I see him again. It's the dry season, I'm just then busy picking off the dead leaves and raking, and he throws a note into the yard. I bend down carefully, only after I have raked all the leaves toward that particular corner, and I pretend

I'm picking up a pile of leaves, but meanwhile I pick up the letter from the ground and tuck it into my apron pocket, because I always put an apron on over my clothes when I'm working like that, I have to because of my father. I wait first, and then I go around to the back, at the end of the yard there's the water closet, dark of course, but here I have the time to unfold the piece of paper and read it. Come at such-and-such a time to this particular place, it says. I know, that's up the hill, there's a waterfall there, too, and lots of pretty plants grow up there, because it's cool, and I've never been there by myself, but I go because of course I'm curious. He's a nice boy, not very big, and a good talker, lots of jokes, we talk a little about this and that, he goes swimming, but I only watch because I've just been sick and I don't want to catch cold, and he walks me back home, not to the gate, because he's scared of my father, who is Prussian, after all, far and wide everybody knows he's strict, very strict, so that's why. . . *Adú!* My father shakes me, 'Where have you been?' he asks. He whacks me with his belt. So many times. And then I have to pull down my pants, my underpants, so strange. He looks between my legs. I don't know why. Later I know that he's afraid that I'm not pure anymore, of course, but I'm innocent, and that boy, too, and yet I'm not allowed to go off the premises ever by myself anymore, after that, I always have to have my brothers or sisters or a girl friend with me as a chaperone."

I started liking him. The first time I thought it was peculiar, that man's panting and all that sweat on his forehead and body, the wrinkles in his face that got deeper just before he shouted out his orgasm. And I stared in amazement at his erection, because his penis, for the first time the Latin name linked up to what I was seeing, appeared to be sculpted, no, in my hand it seemed plastic. In any case it startled me because for a second I thought that he was a woman who had had an operation, so I pinched and poked at the thing to know for sure there was blood inside. A lot of the time I was angry at the things he said, and he'd laugh, "What pain lurks beneath this rage?"

He was also at my birthday party. David spoke to my family as if he had known them for years, but in the same fashion as he ran his seminars. He posed questions, and if people hesitated in their response, he would point out the resistance they had to overcome, and the boy, already four by then, who had met him a few times before without ever wanting to say anything to him as if to be loyal to his father that way, said, "He wants to know everything about everybody else, but he doesn't ever say anything about himself."

David said, "Your mother shuts all her passions up behind an embittered mouth. Watch out that you don't get to be like your mother, don't let yourself be frustrated." And I think that with these words he pulled me into his bed.

After three months I wanted to stop. Martin had started to see the seriousness of it and asked me to come on a long trip. But David wouldn't just let me go. He booked the same trip and left his students behind. "A sabbatical," he called the two months he followed us around Asia. The entire trip I kept trying to free myself of him, but he would keep entangling me with his words.

Thanks to David I learned to talk about all those things in my childhood about which I never talked, subjects that Martin wasn't allowed to touch, that I'd rather not write about now either, even though I know I should. And it was precisely through David that I understood Martin better, in any case never again complained about the burned evidence.

• • •

Actually, Grandma, actually I was never—except with Neo, that's true, that was wrong, lowdown, and dishonest—unfaithful to Martin. Nico, Michiel, Jeff, Oscar, Ronald, Knut, Goert, Manuelo, Haim, Gurtu, and what's his name that French guy I ran into in Tokyo in a bathroom, because of a broken lock on the door and with whom I spent hours talking next to a stinking toilet, Harun, Claudio, I'm afraid I've forgotten a few, Sagon, Kees, Marty, Enrico, Anthony, Pablo, that pilot in Karachi, that Japanese guy in San Francisco, that poet in Budapest, I had no choice.

VIII

I called, she answered. "This is Lieve," a painful name as it means dear, sweet, beloved but Neo says that three-quarters of the Flemish population is called Lieve, and that he didn't make up the name.

In the beginning there was only the ribbon, I became drunk with his scent, I sniffed in the air he breathed out, lay my fists in his armpits, not a second was lost laying his skin against mine, our heartbeat one. Neo scrunched up on my lap, in my arms like a little boy, sucked on my breasts just like a child. Never was an embrace more peaceful than ours. I would stroke his stomach, his flat buttocks that were too wide, his short back. His kiss was like the first one, his mouth swallowed up my vulva, my vaginal lips, my thick black pubic hair; his skin was soft like a child's beneath my fingertips.

Only later did he become a man like the others, no more patience in his tongue, his hands not searching and discovering anymore, but already knowing where my body stops and starts.

I miss our ribbon, I miss the longing, I miss our covert

happiness.

It was my intention to write a book, not a letter, and to begin with Boy, who taught me the ribbon, the itch of his breath beside my ear, and also the longing for what was forbidden. Why do I feel what I feel, and why is his hand on my breast irksome tomorrow and a pleasure today?

"Those slaps I gave you all were really meant for your father," my mother said.

I had heard from an Indies girl friend that her father had thrown hot soup over her legs, and that he went at them with a hot poker. My red welts I could cover up for a few days with knee socks, a blouse with long sleeves, and then they disappeared again, nobody needed to know about that at school, but that girl's scars never went away.

Almost everybody hit. Generally I didn't know why.

I only saw you lash out once. Obviously you have forgotten it. Aunt Divette's oldest daughter came home with a little packet of stamps. She was seven, a year younger than I was. She had stolen it, egged on by our cousins, from a department store. Lotte and I had been there, but we hadn't noticed anything. She showed us her treasure when she left the store, and I walked home feeling remorse. Should I have gone back, should I turn her in to the police? My mother's Jiminy Cricket was hopping up and down in my stomach.

"Look, Grandma, a present," she said.

"Where did you get that?"

"Found it."

A slap on the mouth, just with the bare hand, maybe not hard, but everybody including our cousins felt the force of it in their faces. It was dead silent in the kitchen. Then you said, gently, "You know I don't like people lying."

Aunt Fuut, Boy's grandmother, was a lot stricter. She hit with anything she could lay her hands on, not only wooden spoons, a *sapulidi* or a switch, but also a coathanger, a shoe, an umbrella, a cane, whatever was handy.

I don't know if Boy had scars. Downstairs at Grandpa and Grandma van Maldegem's, in the big room next to Aunt Yossa's, with the narrow dark little corridor leading down to it, where Aunt Fuut lived with her husband, Grandpa Prince, there was no poker or hot soup. My grandmother, who cooked for everyone, always had soup ready over the pilot light of the stove for anybody who wanted to have some, but that soup was lukewarm, you couldn't get burns from that. Besides, Aunt Fuut never hit Boy right in front of us like my mother who, in her rage, couldn't care less if the entire neighborhood saw and heard. Aunt Fuut would pull Boy downstairs by the ear, and if we listened well at the top of the stairs we could find out with what she was beating his back, legs and head. I held my breath and thought, "Oh, good, the *sapulidi*," or, "Oh, no, Grandpa Prince's belt."

Sometimes Boy stayed with his grandmother and grandfather, whom he called Mums and Pops, for just about half the year and the other half he lived with his mother, who was single, but exactly what the situation was, nobody wanted to say.

My oldest cousin, who really wasn't a real cousin because Aunt Fuut was one of Grandpa van Maldegem's sisters, did everything on the sly because everything, even tag or hide-and-seek, was forbidden. When Aunt Fuut was bathing in the bathroom, Boy would point at one of us and say, "You're It," at

163

which we all noiselessly found a place. Boy would hide to-gether with me, close against each other behind the door or in a closet. Hide-and-seek was more fun with him around, and we'd pinch each other's mouths shut to stifle our giggling. From all the different corners of the house we paid attention to the sounds in the bathroom. When we couldn't hear the water running anymore, we would wait anxiously, close to the dining room into which the bathroom door opened out, and rush out of our hiding places as soon as we recognized the first click of the lock on the bathroom door.

When she came out with wet thin lanky black hair, cut each week at her request by Grandpa Prince right above her ears, and parted on the side as straight as a ruler, always with the same dress on that was far too big, a towel over her arm, holding a pair of men's shoes in her hand that Boy was supposed to pol-ish for her, and saw us sitting at the table snickering behind our hands, puzzles and gin-rummy sanctimoniously scattered among the breakfast dishes, she would lay her hand on Boy's forehead, feel that it was damp, that he was sweaty, and cru-elly yank him up from the table and out of the room by the ear.

I thought she was a witch, because she was so skinny that she looked like a skeleton, because she walked hunched over, because she wore tent dresses that came down to her ankles and thick gray men's socks in men's shoes, because she almost never talked, except when she uttered incomprehensible incantations in a hushed but peppery tone while punishing Boy. All Grandma Charlotte's grandchildren refused to call Aunt Fuut, Grandma Prince. Even Aunt Prince we thought was an inap-propriate name for that old woman that we feared.

It was nice to get up on Grandpa Prince's lap. During the day he went to work, and we saw Aunt Fuut only at breakfast, when she went into or came out of the bathroom. Grandma Charlotte made sure that we greeted her each morning with,

"Good morning, Aunt Fuut," even though we preferred to stay out of her way. Grandma Charlotte herself never spoke to her. I am sure that in all those years that Aunt Fuut and Grandpa Prince lived with them I never saw them talking.

In the evening they were the first ones at the table. Aunt Fuut prayed aloud, mumbling ten Hail Marys and ten Our Fathers. Grandma Charlotte always put a big pitcher of water and lots of glasses on the table. Grandpa Prince would fill three glasses when Boy was there, one for each of them, even when Lotte and I had already slipped into our chairs beside them at the oval table. Aunt Fuut would place seven pills beside Grandpa Prince's plate, three green ones, three red ones and one white one. In Boy's hand she would put two green ones, one red one and one big brown calcium tablet that he was supposed to swallow down immediately with the water. The little jars with the pills stood next to the bird cage on top of the tall refrigerator the rest of the day. When they had finished their plates, they prayed again, the same number of Hail Marys and Our Fathers. Aunt Fuut would wipe her mouth with her napkin and disappear into the toilet while Grandpa Prince took their plates to the kitchen, put them in the sink and washed them. If Aunt Fuut were done first she would stand and wait in front of the toilet door, her bent body motionless, as she once more wiped her chin with her napkin. Then they would steal to their room downstairs.

If Grandpa Prince were done first he would pat me or Lotte on the head and do magic tricks with a quarter, cough, blow his nose, until Aunt Fuut came out of the bathroom and he would follow her down the stairs. When Boy was there he was sent to the full bathroom directly after dinner, and Aunt Fuut, after having used the toilet, would sit without moving in front of the bathroom door on a wooden stool used by Grandpa Manus for hanging the cages, and wait like a lackey until Boy reappeared smelling strongly of toothpaste. Although he was a lot older than we were he had to go to bed every evening at seven o'clock, even when he was already fourteen.

At the stroke of seven the two old people would come upstairs again. There were two chairs we were not allowed to sit in after a few minutes to seven. Grandma Charlotte would set out coffee for them in special mugs. Grandpa Prince would occasionally make jokes. Sometimes he would do magic tricks with a handkerchief and a dime, or with playing cards so that he would keep pulling the Jokers out of the pack I had just shuffled. He would pull me up onto his lap, blow on my neck, almost in a whisper sing Malaysian songs in my ear, read my palm, his fingers seeking out the lines, "You're going to get married, you're going to be rich and you're going to get everything your little heart desires," or ask me to help him do his crosswords. He had books full of puzzles, and filled in one after the other. Aunt Fuut did nothing. She just stared off and now and then she would wipe her handkerchief over her mouth, as if something itched, her lips tightly together as if she were scared that her mouth might otherwise accidentally start talking all by itself.

Sometimes Boy would venture to sneak upstairs and play a game of goose or Scrabble in absolute secrecy. He would lift me off my chair and take me on his lap, or slip into the same chair beside me, ready to run away, sitting on the very edge. Whenever Aunt Fuut found out she would let him have it.

Grandma Charlotte would brood resentfully in the kitchen whenever we pricked our ears to hear whether Boy were going to survive his punishment, "She was never a child herself."

I once asked Aunt Yossa, "Was Aunt Fuut really never a child?"

"No, she was born an old woman."

"And Grandpa Prince? Was he a child?"

"He was fun before he got to know that witch, he used to be just like Boy."

"Can Aunt Fuut die just like other people?"

"No, she'll grow a tail and turn into a devil."

Somebody, an uncle I didn't know very well, who also kept birds, came to see Grandpa, kept his winter jacket on during his visit, pinched my cheeks, pulled my chin up toward his face, eyeballed me and said, "Manus, this little one looks like your sister Fuut." I was already able to read and write, wasn't yet ten, I think. I was slender, that's true, thin, just like Aunt Fuut, and that very day I got my hair cut in a pageboy just like the Dutch girls at school by Grandma's hairdresser. Grandpa must have seen my shocked face. He reassured me, "When she was still little, he means."

"Not true," I said angrily, panicking, filled with indignation, but mostly filled with the fear that I might some day be like her, "Aunt Fuut was never little."

And then both men laughed.

My cousins said that my mother was strict. "Your mother's like Aunt Fuut."

And it was a little bit true, Grandma, my mother seemed to be more her daughter than yours, because my mother didn't use any make-up either, kept her hair short because she couldn't stand tickly little wisps of hair on her forehead or in her neck, always dressed in the same formless dresses, lashed out with whatever she could grab and was the only one of your daughters who defended her, "Aunt Fuut isn't bad, she's just afraid that Boy is going to come to a bad end because her only daughter already took a wrong step."

I don't know why I'm writing you about Grandpa's nasty sister.

· · ·

After all, you weren't fond of her either, I don't need to tell you anything. You hardly ever showed that you were annoyed with or critical of her behavior, but your silence said more than you could have told us. It relieves me to write about her and through my own words I realize that Boy was my first love. I couldn't talk yet when, pressed against him, holding my breath—neither he nor I moved—I discovered the ribbon that I had forgotten due to all my mother's boos.

His pain was my pain.

Watching was worse than feeling.

My Grandpa was strict with the boys, but not with us. Or were Lotte and I never naughty? While I'm writing this, I'm recalling that the girls sometimes got slapped, too, but Lotte and I must have been too scared to be naughty. My mother would punish us more, hit harder than Grandpa, if she knew that we, as she said, "had brought her shame."

We had to prove that she had married a man who was intelligent, who knew how to go about things, who was good enough to be his son-in-law. We spoke with two words, we cleaned up our toys and those of the others, helped do the dishes, sat with our arms folded when Grandpa was listening to the news on the radio, and stuck to the rules my mother had laid down. Every vacation we showed her good report cards with good grades, we won medals in athletics, let him win at chess, and didn't comment when he altered the rules of the game whenever he was losing.

Grandpa hit the boys with a bamboo slat or made them pump. Hands at their ears they had to do deep knee bends, a hundred times, and he'd tap his bamboo slat on the glass table, "And a one, two, three, and a one, two, three," so that they wouldn't let the tempo lag.

Aunt Manda was sweet, not strict. She swatted at her sons with her soft slippers, threw her red velvet slippers after them, and warned, "Don't let it happen again!" She intervened, she said, so that Uncle Didi wouldn't notice that they'd been bad, because her husband hit them harder, more severely and was unsparing, even when she herself asked him to relent. He made the boys get the switch which was kept in the corner of the toilet next to the bottles, themselves, and if they refused he would beat and kick them forward until, on their knees, they reached the toilet where he would wield the switch and we could hear the boys scream. Usually the oldest had to be the first, and it was very rare that only one of them was punished, while the others hid in the cramped children's playroom with their Matchbox cars and tin soldiers to stay out of the way until their father's rage had subsided. Lotte and I would run after them, behind the ranting uncle and the little cousin, our fingers in our ears, but still wanting to see whether he wasn't going to beat the boy to death. Not wanting to look and yet feeling compelled to look because imagining is worse.

The switch sometimes whizzed right past my face. I concentrated on the ink-spewing eyes of my uncle who stepped on our feet, ran us down, and if my aunt slipped in between, would threaten her as well with his fist or with the switch that quivered in the air.

There are moments that I can't speak anymore, and then I have to pay attention to my breathing and eating, then I have to clamp everything in me that is open shut, my mouth, my ears, my eyes, and also my navel, and the openings in my crotch. The pain begins in my vagina, at my Kasesa that I suck in like an animal its tail, and then I try to deaden myself on the outside and only be alive on the inside.

It happened for the first time in Singapore, the first trip Martin and I took; we were walking down the street because we had thirty-six hours before the next flight would bring us to Indonesia. It was my first day outside of Europe, the first trip without my family, and there was no baby yet. We were standing at a set of lights. An Asian couple, maybe Chinese, but that isn't the point, she was wearing a gray suit, he was wearing jeans with a striped shirt and a light gray jacket, or maybe they were brother and sister, I don't know, but it seemed like a couple the way they were walking and arguing, crossed the street with us. Right in the crosswalk, the man grabbed the woman's thick black hair and pulled her down while he kept walking. The woman moaned in pain, tried to get away, but the man's grip became stronger, then the man accelerated, forcing her into a stooped position because of his grip. She broke down and started crying, in a whimper, but let out a plaintive yelp of distress clearly for the passersby. Nobody responded. On the other side of the street he smacked her hard across the face and again dragged her along by her hair.

I didn't speak for three, four days. I hated every man, but also every woman, every woman who doesn't defend herself, I hated Martin, that he didn't understand that I couldn't tolerate his hand on my thigh after seeing this scene, I hated myself for not stepping in.

My father didn't strike out. My mother would slam down her plate, throw an empty pan on the floor, yell a lot and bellyache even more, would lock herself in the bedroom, but I never saw them actually fight, my parents, I only heard them shout, day in and day out, about little things, quarreling without end.

I did see Aunt Divette fight, at almost every party, usually toward the time that we were going to bed, and then it would start in the kitchen or in the hallway, because she was angry that he was drunk again, that he had tried to feel Aunt Manda's breasts or that he had laid his hand on Aunt Eva's backside. Grandpa would try to hush the couple. They would be separated. She would sleep upstairs with us, beside us on the mattresses, and he would sleep downstairs somewhere with the others, or he'd sleep it off on the dining room floor because he sometimes flailed out when they wanted to pick him up. "It's the alcohol," said my mother, "he can't handle it."

"You two were never really naughty," said my mother, "But I didn't want anyone to be able to criticize anything about you." She was straightforward, not back-handed like Aunt Fuut, and hit us only when we broke her rules. The times that she was cheerful, that the sun was shining, that her lips curled into a smile and that her eyes shone, she would only once lightly slap my cheek at some infraction, like you did, Grandma, that one time you slapped my niece on the mouth for stealing the stamps and let me go. But generally, especially in the winter, she didn't seem to be able to stop. There was always some reason: I never managed to walk into the kitchen at five o'clock sharp and I was always putting a jar of peanut butter or the cookie tin back in the wrong place, often I'd been too eager for the chocolate or for the *spekkoek*, I was in a hurry or shy and said hello rudely, thoughtlessly brought in dirt on my shoes, had torn my dress climbing a tree, through carelessness had forgotten to close the door behind me, got jam on the carpet in my greed, or had accidentally let the faucet in the bathroom run; and after the first whack there was always sufficient exasperation so that I'd wildly slam the doors, or kick a chair on purpose, and then she would start flat out pounding away.

In retrospect she says she was too strict, that she came down on us too hard, but that she had been cooling her anger on us over what had been unfair in her life, as soon as we, who were obedient children really, gave her reason to by, for instance, coming home five minutes late. But I'm losing track here. Why am I burdening you with all of this? You often pet our heads and said, "That's just how your mother is. She's hot-tempered. She got that from Grandpa Manus and Grandma Virginia, that's the mixture of the Madurese and the Fleming, and then the Prussian from my father on top of that. . . . What can you expect? Everybody's got their character."

Aunt Manda didn't seem like she could ever get angry. She would give her sons the house keys, make twenty sandwiches and send them off to the park while she went to the cinema to see a Romy Schneider movie. The boys would come home covered with mud, with holes in their shoes because while jumping from boat to boat they'd fallen in the canal, or because they'd been chasing ducks at the pond. She never asked, she didn't complain about the mud all over the floor, but got out a rag and started cleaning, slapdash and fast if Uncle Didi were coming home that evening, taking her time and singing when he was at sea.

I'd rather remember that it always used to be summer.

One day, my boy was still a baby, I told her that I hated her for having hit us, that I would never, but truly never, hit my child, and that she had tried day in and day out to force her will on us as if she thought she could hammer her rules into our veins, into our blood by way of our skin. I said this in a crowded room, with lots of my friends, little family, around and she sat there so frail in a chair that was too big, shrank, shook her head, swallowed, swallowed again, and said loud enough for everybody to hear, "No, I was wrong, but I always got beaten as well and I didn't know any better, thought that was the way it was supposed to be. It was only when I heard other mothers talking, when you were both grown, about how hitting wasn't a common thing for everybody, that I started thinking. And every slap I gave you was actually meant for your father."

It was a relief, Grandma, to tell her in front of all those people what I hadn't dared to in twenty years. But now I'm sorry, because she was right, in all her rules she was right, and everything was meant to protect us from real pain. Her morals, her rules were fair, but I wasn't capable of what she was able to do so easily. On my fortieth birthday she surprised me again, "Why didn't Neo come?"

"He can't," I said, "his wife doesn't want him to."

"That's stupid of her. It's better to go with the wind, because then everything wears off naturally. I've been in love with somebody else once or twice myself, and it wasn't easy for me because your father was never affectionate with me, making love for him is an act that takes a couple of minutes, while as a woman you want a loving touch sometimes too. But when I get to know another man who is attentive to me, who is gallant, then I compare him to your father and see a lot of things that the man doesn't have and your father does, so it isn't so hard to forget my infatuation."

I want to tell you something, but what I'm going to write

has nothing to do with that incident. It seems as though I want to punish myself with memories of things that were black, at your house, at my aunts', and in my mother's house, for what I don't dare to write, for what is unforgivable, what I don't believe when I write you and which you must forget faster than anything else I have noted down for you.

I wanted to remain innocent like Aunt Manda, a little bit blind, but very happy when I dance. I wanted to horse around and never lose, like Aunt Yossa. I wanted to be the wisest, like you, but didn't have the capacity to remain silent. From fear of being my mother, or worse still, an Aunt Fuut, I missed out on free will.

Martin and Neo were talking about the car while I took her on, his Lieve, who had brought their daughters over to her parents' that afternoon to be able to receive us undisturbed.

I would rather blame him and see myself as the victim. Looking back, everything seems to have been orchestrated by him. But he, too, is innocent. We made an attempt to be straightforward, we wanted to better our lives, but still didn't know how to. We talked of the Trobriand Islands, hadn't booked the trip yet, and discussed it like a dream that didn't have to become reality. Martin started getting restless, he wanted to get to know Lieve, he had said. Every time Neo called or came to visit he would ask, "When are we finally going to get to meet your wife?"

I was curious, but also scared.

He called out of the blue. "What would you two think if I were to show you some First World War trenches? That should interest you, Martin, being an anthropologist, how those young boys your son's age lived there for years. And at the same time you can get acquainted with my wife."

"Those trenches I can do without, really," Martin told me, "but it's time we met his Lieve."

We shook each other's hands, and she wouldn't meet my gaze. I searched her eyes. She averted them. I counted the cigarettes in the ashtray that she had smoked in silence. Fourteen. Neo and I had known each other exactly fourteen weeks.

He shifted until he touched her, his thigh almost brushing hers when he leaned forward to pass Martin the milk, and for a brief moment he leaned lightly against her upper arm.

Neo and I had been together a lot already, just the two of us, his body was already mine, his heartbeat mine, and now I was seeing him sitting next to a stranger with whom he was more one that with me. The naturalness of their actions, the objects they handed to one another, the wear in the leather of the couch, two spots, their backsides worn in. I undressed them, pictured her in a white bra and white lace panties standing by the bathroom sink and saw him in his tight cotton briefs scratching his balls, watching as she unfastened her bra and carefully draped the small garment over the chair. They had never taken a bath together, he had once said when he had booked a suite for us in a fancy hotel as a surprise, because he'd always dreamed of that, of some day lying in a tub with a woman like me the way they do in the movies, the champagne beside you on a cart, a basket of fruit, caviar and twice-baked potatoes with sour cream, and then, our skin soggy, we sat with Martin at the kitchen table, went on about how we had eaten fries and herring, weren't hungry anymore, and I had to go lie down because we'd walked on the beach, for miles, yes, from IJmuiden eight-and-a-half miles to Zandvoort, the weather had been nice, no the rain hadn't been too bad.

She echoed everything he said, indifferently; suddenly he

and Martin had no topics of conversation anymore, every attempt faltered, and in a last ditch effort Martin, who never cared about cars, asked about the Cadillac, what year, how many cylinders, how many horses, what about replacing parts, what does it run on, how many miles on it. . . . In the meantime I guessed at her full breasts under the black dress, a plain cut, restrained, well-bred, like her gestures and her striking make-up which was severe rather than provocative and yet attractive due to the beauty mark on her left cheek.

I wanted to hate her or like her, but not to be indifferent. Her nails, painted the color of her lips, rubbed me the wrong way, and I was glad to see something that I disliked.

"There were only 532 Eldorados manufactured in that year."

His voice sounded proud.

Martin kept up with his questions, showed interest. It was as if they were talking about a woman, a celebrity, when Neo described the exceptional parts and body that characterized the car. English terms among the Flemish, because in Lieve's presence his vocabulary and his accent had become more Flemish than before. He looked to Lieve for confirmation in order to attest to the unique aspects and particularly the beauty of this 50s specimen in comparison to the many other models that had been produced around the same period, and which both had seen at auctions, in private ownership, at collectors', in search of this one authentic one.

Panoramic windshields

Metal trunk

Folding convertible top

The luxury car of luxury cars

The good life

High class

A world standard

I said something unkind, "What kind of a poem is that? Or

is it prose? James Joyce? Dylan Thomas? Must be a Brit, or is it an American?"

Martin looked peeved. I disappeared into the bathroom. I shouldn't have gone, I wanted to leave this strange, large house, hide myself.

He was waiting for me in the hall, appeared from some odd corner of the house, pushed me against the wall, pushed his tongue inside my mouth, and I fought free, "Don't, quit it."

"You hit me," he said hurt, his hand rubbing his cheek.

I hadn't noticed, Grandma, it had happened, and I didn't know it. I was shaking, I pushed him aside and whispered, concerned, "They must have heard us."

He kissed me again, I didn't fight anymore, but for an instant everything seemed to be over.

That night we met each other secretly for several minutes in the hall, like children, our hands everywhere, wild, he was seeking passion perhaps, I was seeking the ribbon and the innocence that went with it.

Over breakfast I was surprised by her child's face. Without make-up she looked like my mother, her lips thin and tightly pressed together, her eyes full of suspicion, and she quibbled about everything with Neo, who did his best to keep the mood cheerful by rapping Shakespeare sonnets, which he and Martin had done a lot better some weeks before during our walk in the dunes.

But I felt sorry for her, suddenly saw the absurdity of the whole business, couldn't swallow, couldn't talk, wanted to lay my arm around her shoulder, and say, "Lieve, I'm sorry, I've been wrong, and I'll never do it again."

. . .

I won't defend myself. It isn't any excuse. I ask for mercy, without a word, from you, who forgets and doesn't judge. I can't even honestly say, if the situation were to occur again in the same way, whether I would act differently. It's the animal in me that I can't seem to keep under control. Or maybe it's the only way to escape from the pressure of being a way I don't want to be, and therefore I became another.

I still don't dare, Grandma, I'm working up my courage and will tell you everything, that I promise, but first I'm going to give Kasesa a shower and clean the cage. The bird usually climbs into the cage by itself and won't go out, even if I open the door and place the popcorn and cooked rice in a dish on the counter. Only when I take out the perches and hang them in the kitchen does the bird come out. I play with it for a little while, tickle its neck, behind its head, take it out into the yard, talk to it, because I've left it alone too much. Now and then it plucks out its own feathers. I want to call my son, whether he's recuperated from the party, because he'd had too much to drink and go kiss Martin, tell him that I love him, pull him off his chair, maybe by tearing his shirt to shreds, unzip his fly, and let my cold hand slide in. I want to take him away from his word processor, interrupt his sentences, let him know that I exist, let him feel that I'm alive.

IX

Young boys in black-and-white, in the snow, the remains of people in a tree, six pairs of eyes directed at the camera, asking, "Why?"

On the way there Neo had driven slowly, and we had all sung along with his CDs, sixties hits whose words Martin usually knew best. The sun was bright, and with the top down it seemed like summer, and we all seemed to be friends the way we—Lieve, too—were all boisterously singing. Neo had made a schedule for the day. We were to begin with the photographs, dozens of wooden stereoscopic boxes on a long table in which a war I know little about has been commemorated with the aid of three-dimensional photographs.

Clouds shielded us from the sun as Neo parked the car, and inside it was winter. An electric heater glowed; a woman with a sad expression on her face was sitting in a chair staring off into the distance beside a shiny new racing bike leaning against the timeworn wall. There was a bar with a fat gray-haired man in grubby dress, stains on his shirt, beer foam on his upper lip, tending it, with whom we could change money since each stereo-box cost a token.

Already at the second box Martin said to me under his breath, "I'm not sure I really want to see this."

Lieve sat down in a chair beside the lady near the heater and smoked a cigarette. Now and then Neo said, "Lieve, look," and then she would get up out of the folding chair, slowly walk over to him, and look. "Hmmmm," she would comment.

"Awful, isn't it?"

"Yes, awful," she would respond, and go back to her chair beside the heater with her coat on her lap.

At one photograph, Martin lingered, motionless, and when I peered into that box after him I went down the series twice to figure out which photograph he had stopped and looked at for so long. Among the many photos I saw one of a young soldier who, one leg higher than the other, was obviously posing, one hand on his hip, and behind him lay a corpse, or someone wounded. The contrast between the one posing and the other who might well have been helplessly bleeding to death or died already, maybe stinking, must have made a deep impression on Martin.

After the photos, the cemetery was scheduled. The sun came out again. The white crosses looked whiter. There were lots of people. A British couple laid flowers on a grave, along with a photograph in a frame.

"You know how much I would have wanted a son with you," Neo whispered when Martin and Lieve had already strolled off and we were still looking at the elderly lady as she arranged a ribbon with "My dear Father" printed on it in black letters around the framed picture of a young man not even twenty. "But you know, right now I'm very happy I only have daughters."

We toured the trenches, skipping a little museum where Lieve waited because she didn't want to walk in the mud with her shoes. Neo tapped the walls, "All exactly like it was then, those sandbags. Can you imagine being here for months with the enemy not even three hundred feet away?"

In Vietnam, through the subterranean corridors where the Viet Cong had hidden for years and from which they had operated in their resistance to the Americans, Martin and I had walked as tourists. The first extended trip on which our boy had elected not to go and had instead gone camping with friends in Europe. A fifty-year-old skinny Vietnamese doctor, who had led Martin around and accompanied him to all his interviews, had told us how he, as a young doctor, had performed operations in the tunnels at night, and during the day sat by the water with his comrades supposedly fishing, taking turns to watch that the Americans didn't figure out that they were sleeping, for then they would be suspicious.

The older doctor crawled ahead, I was behind him, and Martin who, with his big Dutch body, had little freedom of movement, got stuck in one of the corridors. Panicking, he had discarded his camera and money pack in order to move faster, and had tried to find us, sweating and gasping for breath, "I'm suffocating," he had called out, "I can't get any air." A Vietnamese boy, I thought he was our son's age, but he turned out to be older, told us that he had been born there and that he had never been above ground during the earliest years of his childhood. He spoke English. On account of his limited vocabulary he sounded breezy, manifesting a remarkable clarity that moved us when he spoke of the death of his parents and his older sister. While the doctor crawled on hands and knees in search of Martin's valuables, we sat in the dark space on the well-swept hard ground, glued to each other. Right next to us we noticed a somewhat roomier area to which we wanted to drag our hot, tired bodies, when the boy pointed, in warning, so it seemed, "Booby trap." In fright we shrank back, at which he smiled reassuringly, showing his teeth, "No more, no more," and I thought of our child, of Martin, of us, of our being helplessly human.

In one of the trenches Martin grabbed me without a word and I was bothered by his grip. I must have known that he was thinking of our child who wasn't a child anymore, who is living on his own, and at that moment I didn't want to be a mother.

"Now we're going to the German cemetery."

"Do we have to?" I asked.

"Of course," said Neo, "don't you think, Martin? We can't skip that. The war wasn't those poor boys' choice, either."

A totally different kind of cemetery, sober, ensconced among the trees, well away from the world, with "Die Eltern," mother and father, especially the father, well, the mother, too, no, just the mother. . . both, side-by-side like that. We fell silent.

"She is a great artist, Käthe Kollwitz," said Neo, "isn't it so, Lieve, we went to Berlin together and saw her work in the Käthe Kollwitz Museum, very impressive. I had in mind doing something with her drawings, and found a poet, somebody of caliber, but the project didn't work out."

Neo talked fast.

Martin said nothing.

He walked hunched up like the statue of the man, his arms folded, his shoulders raised slightly.

"What's the matter?"

Neo had turned his mirror so that he could see my face.

Lieve was wearing sunglasses, Martin had wrapped his scarf around his head and looked pitiful.

"Is it cold back there?"

I thought it was fine, the wind that cleansed my head, the hair that flew in all directions, the goose bumps on my arms.

"It's chilly," said Martin.

"Shall I put the top up?"

"No," I said, "down, please."

Martin coughed and pulled the woolen scarf tighter around his neck.

"Are you cold, Lieve?"

She shook her head, no. She was wearing an ochre winter coat without a collar, a fur stole wrapped around her head and neck.

"In front you're protected from the wind," said Neo.

"The panoramic windshields." Martin coughed his remark at Neo's back.

"There's a throw in the back, there, on the floor, put that around yourself."

Martin eagerly looked on the floor and found a big heavy blanket that he bundled around himself, until he was wrapped from head to toe.

"Is that better?"

"Yes, much better." Martin sat huddled, and because of his expression, I wondered if he were studying Neo, who kept fixing his eyes on my face by means of the wide mirror while he was driving. Martin's face was pale, maybe from the cold, maybe from the day, from all the death that lurked behind the cracks of the graves. I snuggled against him and he immediately threw the blanket around me as well in such a matter-of-fact manner that I backed away in surprise because I, hmm, it's strange, isn't it, Grandma, it surprises me, I feel ashamed, maybe even more of this than of what happened later. . . I freed

183

myself from his grasp, because I thought it was painful for Neo.

At that moment, or ten seconds later, Neo said, as he shifted his gaze in the rearview mirror discreetly from me then pointedly to Martin, "Would you mind taking over the wheel for a little while?"

Martin was silent.

Neo stepped on the brake, repeated his question, "Would you like to drive? Then you can tell your son that you raced through Belgium in his dream-mobile, he'll think that's beautiful."

"I'd do that," Lieve threw in. Her voice is heavy, an attractive voice, except when she's arguing, then she sounds cold and her mouth hardens. "I have never seen Neo allow anybody behind the wheel. You'd be the first, so you'd better grab your chance before he changes his mind."

Martin shifted his weight, slid forward onto the edge of the seat and pulled the blanket tighter around himself. "Well, you did say it was warmer up front, right?"

They changed places. Martin threw the blanket on the back seat and got comfortable behind the wheel.

"Here, put this on."

Out of the dashboard, Neo took a crumpled up navy blue lamb's wool sweater. Martin flushed. His fingers slid over all the knobs and levers. Leaning on his shoulder, Neo hung over him briefly to explain a few things, but Martin had evidently been paying close attention on the previous excursions.

When Neo sat back on the seat beside me and unfolded the large blanket, shook it and laid it over us, securing it here and there with a few tote bags and other things, I knew what was going to happen. In the rectangular frame of the rearview mirror I saw no more than Martin's chin as he inched his way down the emergency lane to get a feel for the car, carefully checked his visual field, investigated the play in the wheel,

tested the brakes, accidentally honked and in alarm consequently flicked on the windshield wipers, and asked, "What
would you say to Rachmaninoff?" With Lieve's help he put on
Vespers, then he turned the lever of the side view mirror with
no results, and complained, "I can't see in that round thing,
what a bizarre side mirror, Neo, not too much of a panoramic
view unfortunately, is it original too?"

"Everything's authentic about the love of my life," said Neo.
"Step on it so Caddy'll get us out of here, this isn't the most
picturesque landscape in Flanders."

Neo's hand found its way to my breasts, my legs, and carefully his fingers sought that one negligible little spot, that grew
beneath his finger moving slowly, barely perceptibly, but sufficiently for me, and inconspicuously for the others, so that I
could do nothing but lean my head back, feel the back of the
seat against my shoulders, let myself slip down, slide, hidden
behind their seat because of the wind, so it appeared, I think,
to Lieve and Martin, who were listening to the music we
couldn't hear in the back.

X

It fascinated Neo that Kasesa preferred to remain in the cage, and also that the cockatoo he had known as a big talker never wanted to say anything anymore. He had bought the bird from a billionaire, whose wife had wanted to sell it long before, from the moment her husband had become paralyzed on one side by a stroke, but who had until then found none of the dealers trustworthy. Neo told anecdotes in which the parrot had made its voice heard at precisely the right moment.

During a banquet with a minister of state at mention of an oral—illegal—agreement, the bird had cried, "Stop that thief." And during the visit of a thorough tax inspector who, as he was going through the papers, stumbled upon a bothersome question and by means of an unbearable silence had made it clear that he desired an immediate answer to his exacting inquiry, the cockatoo, while its owner was dutifully searching for an answer that would be acceptable for the moment, had screeched in its shrill voice, "See you." The billionaire, made slightly more confident by the inspector's fit of laughter, seeing the mood had lightened, ventured an attempt at an arrangement by means of a hearty handshake with success.

And then again when Neo, "in all honesty, just before I got to know you at the gallery," had gone by himself to visit the billionaire to deliver some special editions he had ordered some time before, found the wife at home alone and she had let him know indirectly that he was more than welcome now that her husband was in the hospital due to a second stroke, and the cockatoo had saved the situation with, "Not now, babe," at which their laughter had made all the painful tension of the moment vanish.

Lieve had always been crazy about the bird. They had been stopping by to see these particular acquaintances for about twelve years, and the husband had helped him a few times with business matters. "Meisje, promise me that she'll never know that I gave Kasesa to you as a present," he said, and it was better to pretend that we had gotten to know one another when Martin and I had gone to Belgium, to the province of Limburg to buy the bird, and he had by chance been visiting at the spacious villa. Lieve would have liked to have had the cockatoo, but he hadn't considered it a good idea, "A cockatoo takes up too much time and that won't work out with so many demanding daughters."

My father determined what was and wasn't to be purchased. My mother had no money of her own, just managed to make ends meet with the household money and observed with resignation how her husband bought himself a new linen suit while she had been making do with the same winter coat for twenty years. He became furious when he found out that she had bought on credit at the green grocer's.

"How is it possible that a sergeant-major who lives on the same street as we do has a car and a television, and I, as an adjutant, for goodness' sake, can't buy anything because you're always making debts!"

"Who's always so glad to eat my *saté kambing?*" she retorted. "What do you think the *spekkoek* costs that you like so much? Go sit down to dinner with that sargeant-major, who only eats potatoes and half a pork-roll, who sends his guests home before dinner on empty stomachs, and who lets his friends come to celebrate his birthday only after eight, when they've already eaten their fill at home so he only has to present them with coffee and a cookie. Then you'd also save enough to buy a television!"

She couldn't go to the play put on by the Catholic parish because she couldn't afford to take a couple of dollars out of the household money, but he bought an expensive camera which he kept in its box with the Styrofoam among his underwear and socks in the closet, because he thought the instructions were too difficult to read. She complained that she still didn't have a washing machine and that her fingers had been worked to the bone on the washboard on which she scrubbed our dirty clothes, and he shouted, "You got spoiled by the good life, the colonial days are over, everybody washes their clothes themselves, you married a sergeant, and it was pretty good that I was able to work my way up to being an adjutant, but you only want to live like some general's wife."

When I was eleven I sent a poem in to a school contest and won first prize. It got published in the school paper and I got "The Big Summer Vacation Book," which I didn't let my parents see to avoid their getting to know anything about the poem, but the chaplain came to our house to ask if I might not read "the poem about money" in church.

I looked for it later among my old essays, diaries and verses on loose sheets of paper, in notebooks and pads, in a big chest in the attic, and in strayed folders and boxes. Actually I've always saved everything, but when my boy got older, he got my workroom in the attic and I moved my things into his, which is much smaller, and during that move notes and pads must have gotten mislaid. Since he has left the house and I've nestled myself back into the attic, there hasn't been an opportunity to sort everything out. (While looking for the poem I ran across all kinds of other sheets of paper and letters of whose existence I had forgotten. That's what I'd like to tell you about, Grandma, because I think it's important.) The following two lines from the poem I still remember: "Money straightens that which is crooked. And money makes crooked that which could have been straight."

There was another text I was supposed to read after my poem and the chaplain had typed it out for me in capital letters so that I could rehearse it along with the poem; Matthew 6:25–25: "Therefore I say unto you: Take no thought for your life, what ye shall eat, or what ye shall drink; nor yet for your body, what ye shall put on. Is not the life more than meat, and the body than raiment?'"

My mother was proud of me. On Saturday afternoon my father, as a surprise, bought me a new dress at a sale that I was to wear the next day during mass, at the front of the church, behind the microphone, on a lectern that was bedecked with green felt, to read the text. The dress was wide, of shiny material with green and purple. Not the colors I would have chosen myself, and a little too big, but it was already so unusual that I had gotten a new dress and that the style wasn't totally out-of-date. The chaplain didn't want to pass Lotte by, so she was allowed Matthew 6:31–34, a longer text with the word "righteousness" in it, which she found hard to pronounce properly because she had braces on her upper teeth. She got an orange and blue dress, likewise not her favorite colors, the same style as mine, which did fit right, and she, too, was overjoyed that we wouldn't have to wear Aunt Eva's old dresses for once on Sunday.

In delight we showed my mother the dresses, which we had put on right away, and turned around for her. She said nothing. Lotte started dancing elatedly around the living room and pirouetting around the furniture so that her dress stood out, she practiced the sentence, "But seek ye first the kingdom of God, and his righteousness; and all these things shall be added unto you." In the meantime I sought my mother's eyes. "What's wrong, do you think the dress is ugly?"

She burst into tears, Grandma, and slammed the kitchen door right in my face. I went upstairs and immediately took off the dress, wasn't happy with it anymore, went down to her again as she was frying *kroópook,* standing over the hot oil. I can still see her back, bent, in a nylon flower-print apron with white buttons up the back. I asked her why she was crying and she said, "Your father never thinks of me."

Neo called. I was startled because I had been waiting, hoping for days, and hadn't heard from him at all.

I ran downstairs from the attic, having been absorbed for hours in the letters, essays and poems from my childhood, but especially from my pubescent years, which made me realize that I really haven't changed much since then. I had found poems about my mother, sonnets, of all things, Grandma. Albeit my prosody was rather free in those days, not bound by rules, the poems about her are formally tight and still keenly reflect my relationship to my mother. When I look at the date, it turns out I wrote the poem when I was fourteen. In May, and then I remember exactly when: there had been a fair, and there had been Peter.

It was so funny to hear him say, "Yes, it's me." It had always sounded natural, and now, after being fourteen again for a little while, having kissed Peter, felt Peter's hands under my sweater, not knowing for sure whether he was touching my breasts, but sure that there was a sensation running through my body which, I thought, had to be called happiness, so you don't want to move anymore, to think anymore and you forget everything around you, I was startled older, so for an instant I couldn't recall who he was. It wasn't more than half a second, the silence, but long enough for him to tack on, "Neo. Am I interrupting something?"

"No, not at all."

"It took such a long time for you to answer."

"Yeah, I was upstairs."

"Is Martin home?"

"No, at the university, preparations for his postdoctorate."

"Then what were you doing?"

"Oh, I was reading, things from a long time ago."

"What kinds of things?"

"You know, stories and poems I wrote when I was a kid."

"Are you planning on doing anything with them?"

"No, I was just reading them."

"Fun?"

"Yes, well no, actually not fun, they made me cry."

"Well, then I won't keep you any longer."

"No, I'm happy you called. How's it going? Not having any more arguments with Lieve?"

"We don't talk about it anymore, that's all. But I'm having quite a time with my daughters. How was the party?"

"Oh, I forgot about that. It's been so long ago."

"Were there a lot of people?"

"Yeah, tons."

"Was the music good?"

"Very."

"How did Kasesa react to it, all those people?"

"Oh, Kasesa had a good time."

"Saying anything yet, finally?"

"Yes, that's right, that bird lied for the first time."

Amongst my things I found a crumpled piece of paper that had been torn up. It turned out to be three pieces of unlined airmail stationery with blue ballpoint writing on them, two different styles of handwriting. I took the bits, carefully unfolded them and pressed them flat with my hand, had to unroll snippets folded double carefully, and flatten them, and in so-doing watch that they didn't rip any further, because the puzzle was hard enough to fit together as it was.

I had forgotten, Grandma, and when I showed Martin the pieces, he said right away, "That isn't either of our handwriting." Only when I read him the letter aloud was he prepared to believe that we had really written each other these texts in the winter, just before I got to know Michiel, our boy was almost four, and that he had snatched the sheets out of my hand, ripped them up, crumpled them and tossed them into the waste paper basket, out of which I had fished the wads hours later and without uncrumpling them, had hidden them in my suitcase among the diaries from high school.

After Fernando there had been nobody but Martin. And because of the letter, actually it wasn't a letter, but first a long text in my handwriting, then a response to it from Martin, his steady, legible, masculine handwriting, and then some scribblings without capitals, commas, periods in my own handwriting, I remember someone named Anton, who is mentioned in my text, and therefore also briefly in Martin's, a graduate assistant, twelve years older than I was, divorced father of two, dark expressive eyes, gray hairs among the rich black, with a

192

strong body odor that pleased me, that sometimes made me dizzy. During labs I would with regularity lose track of the conversation because of his presence, but the funny thing was that the excitement I felt at his proximity made me long for Martin, who was seldom at home, traveled a lot, was always writing, and participated in all sorts of committees. Anton wrote me love letters, tossed poems in my mail box, took care of the boy when I was taking the exam, and I started dreading being alone with him much when I noticed that at the concerts and plays he took me to, I yearned to let my head drop into his lap and put his fingers in my mouth.

During that time I must have gotten out of bed at night and gone downstairs to write at the big table in subdued light, the way I was already writing short stories then, too, until far into the night, because there was nobody to distract me.

"At our house he's the one who determines how things are going to happen, how long and where it's going to happen, but especially whether it happens or not. First a frontal remark, 'I want you.' Then I grab him around his waist, at his legs, or around the neck as if have to share him with other women crowding in, I caress him, smell him, shove my nose into his armpit, feel one with him, and then he falls asleep.

"I'm alone. I can't tell everything. Not that I'm thinking of seducing Anton and going to bed with him; I'm still calmly weighing the practical consequences. Not because I want him instead, not because I happen to go for him, but simply because I want some loving.

"Pretty promises: go work somewhere together. But I'm left out in the cold. Not able to sleep, not able to make love. I obviously don't captivate him anymore. Two legs spread apart and wham-bam in ten minutes, that's still OK, but don't start whining again. Tomorrow I'll buy you sweet almond-filled cake and do the dishes, like a liberated man, then you'll know that I love you, that much must be clear.

"I don't need a domestic man, a writer, a journalist, a man with a successful career, an anarchist, a guerrilla fighter, a prophet, a mother who plays boss and takes care of me, I want somebody who loves me, my everything, my body, too.

"You have to think I'm beautiful. You have to want to touch me. My touch has to excite you. You have to want to see me. Want to immerse yourself in me. Not once a month. Each and every night has to be a sensation. I can't even remember the last time it was good.

"I don't want any faking anymore.

"A night's sleep is more productive to you than sperm. And I want nothing else than for somebody to see me. If you don't want to, then somebody else will.

"And yet that isn't it: the appreciation has to come from you if it's to be satisfying. It is torture for me to lie beside you and hear you breathe. I'd rather be jealous of a woman than of abstract sleep. Do you have nice dreams? Is reality coming down a bit too hard on you?

"I can't cry about it anymore. The tears gel on my retina. They blur my vision. Is that supposed to be the point? Am I supposed to keep on going, blindly? Like most people? Like my mother, maybe?

"Enjoy sex.

"You taught me to.

"Did you lose it yourself when you did?

"If that's the case, and if you love me, then you'll still want me to be happy. Maybe you'll advise me to make love to others, go to bed with others.

"Enjoy sex. I still do.

"Don't teach me not to, please.

"Was it then not so wrong of me to be paranoid when you had to retch, Saturday, at my saying with the words that you taught me, because you think it's so much nicer if I spell things out, 'Do you want to fuck me?'

"Was there a purpose in saying that? Do I make you puke? (In any case, physically.)

"I'm alone. I can't talk about this with anybody, because talking with somebody else about you and me would be overstepping the unspoken rule between us. 'Now that's really being unfaithful,' you said once, 'when you start discussing your bedroom secrets with somebody else.'

"And talking with you is impossible. . . .

"I'm happy with my body, I want to use it. If you're not interested anymore, then say so, so that I won't keep waiting around for nothing. I don't want to live dying."

In Martin's handwriting:

"I get your point. But you're driving me crazy. Wasn't it, like Tuesday morning, basically a flop? (Which really bothered me, and still does.)

"I have promised myself that I'll take out enough time the next time. And how am I supposed to know that on Wednesday at 11:30 you think it's early and on Tuesday at 11:30 you say, 'No, not now, I want to sleep.' You don't have any idea how difficult it is when I'm yearning for your body and I feel that I can't give in because afterward it'll turn out that I failed. I really don't know what to do anymore. Maybe you should go to bed with Anton so you'll see that there isn't any difference whatsoever, except that with somebody else there's a lot of tension that gets added in which makes your nerves more sensitive to impressions.

"I don't see any way out to help either myself or you now

that it's becoming so important."

What I remember is that I couldn't speak, my tongue seemed to be glued to the roof of my mouth. While he's talking about splitting up, that he has failed, is obviously worthless, I sit bent over the paper, scratching around with my pen. Inside of me, the scream: I want you, hold me, bite me, take me, lick me from head to toe, devour me, discover me, be me so that for a moment I can be you.

While he paces back and forth in the room, the floor throbs, the boy is asleep, I scribble, up against the edge of the paper in tiny little letters, in an almost illegible handwriting:

"sorry about everything sorry I brought everything up I need you so badly"

He snatches the paper out from under my hands and, unread, rips the three sheets, starts flinging the chairs around, two, against the wall, throws his study books all over the room, leaves the house.

I sit for a long time first, don't move, deliberate whether it's a good idea to disappear, just go, no mess, no blood, no tracks.

Hours later I stand up, stiff, I'm shivering, can hear the wooden floor creak, and search the wastebasket for the crumpled snippets that I quickly shove in among my diaries in a trunk where I save everything from my childhood: before Martin.

I told Anton not to come around anymore. A half year later he got married to somebody whom he has since divorced. I got to know Michiel, then David, then the others.

(Which is strange, Grandma, that Martin and I started making love with more and more passion and with a lot more imagination, in the middle of the day, after a dream in the middle of the night—even when there was somebody else about whom Martin might or might not know—and always with that desperate abandon in our embrace, that for god's sake it won't be the last time, so that we are now, after so many years, looking at the snippets with a frown, feeling pity, compassion for those two young people who didn't understand each other.)

The way my mother skipped through the puddles, that's how I'd like to be now. No clue about the eyes observing her, laughing with her, laughing at her, or put off by the overjoyed girl jumping out of the adult foreign woman. At the house where she was born, where the tall iron gate is shut, the owner isn't home, the servant suspiciously opens up for her, she explains in her Indonesian, which she never spoke well, because she only had to speak with the servants who understood enough Dutch to understand her when she ordered them to polish her shoes or iron her dress, "I am baby in this house, then before." She peeks inside through a window and says, "I don't recognize a thing."

She bites her lip because the tree that her father planted at the time that he buried the placenta isn't there anymore. And the other children's trees have also disappeared, just like the papaya tree whose pit her mother planted when she knew she was pregnant with her, but she had already thought that those fruit trees wouldn't still be growing there anyway.

By the house where she spent the greatest part of her childhood, the fruit tree in which she used to climb regularly with her sister Manda is still standing. She shows me its hard ugly fruit, breaks one open with her teeth, after wiping the skin clean on her cotton blouse and smelling the fruit, takes a bite

197

and says critically, "Mmmm, still too sour," tries to stick a piece in my mouth, chews with relish, but shakes her head, "still not ripe," and eats a second one as if by means of the unripe *jambu,* because it is a *jambu,* I know, a cucumberlike flavor I don't really like very much, she can taste her childhood again.

She runs from one house to the next, points, and calls out, "That's where a Dutch girl lived, there, her mother wouldn't allow her to play outside and we weren't allowed to go into their yard, and Arabs lived over there, you could see veiled women sitting at that little window up there, like prisoners. . . ," while I, sweating, sluggish from the hot city and thirsty because we have been passing by all the places where she had been as a child for hours already, getting into the car, out of the car, squat down on the sidewalk beside a *saté* vendor, look at the red coals, the small flames stirred up by the waving of a fan, missing Martin and our boy, and notice that I'm turning into a mother a little bit, avoiding the smiling eyes, my far too roomy blouse with long sleeves is buttoned up to my chin, long wide pants not to feel the sweat and to avoid anyone's looking at my legs. She has taken off her shoes because they pinch, the pair is next to me on the curb, and at another house where nobody is home, not even any servants, she is trying to climb over the gate just to see if the bougainvillea at the back of the house, that's where her best girl friend used to live, is still there. In visiting her old schools, the various houses where she lived with her family, and in searching for her old friends, I can see myself for the first time in her face.

She has beer with her meals, and never before have I seen her with a glass of alcohol. She asks around at stores, rings strangers' doorbells until she has found her first boyfriend, the only one before she met my father, and teases the fat, bald Chinese man, who owns a store that sells televisions, also secondhand ones that have been taken apart, bits and pieces all over, his house a workshop. She tickles him in his ribs because he says she was the prettiest of the sisters and that she's so white now, which becomes her, that bleached skin from Holland, and that she hasn't changed, hasn't gotten any older, is still as young. "It's been a long time that I spoke Dutch," he says, "my wife doesn't know the language, she only speaks Chinese and speaks Indonesian poorly, she's dumb."

At the market she kisses him spontaneously on both cheeks when he buys her a big wicker basket full of mangosteens. The people standing around laugh and cheer. They shout all kinds of things in Javanese, which I can't understand. She can't either. "I promised you, didn't I, to pick some for you, but unfortunately that didn't ever happen because of the red ants, they were still crawling all over my body hours later." She laughs and as if she were someone else, not my mother, starts telling about how he jumped out of the tree yelling, had taken off his shirt and pants in the middle of the street and in his underwear had stood slapping at all the parts of his body, while he screeched, "*Adú, adú.*" I also got to know his wife, a fat Aunt Fuut, who when we surprised him with our visit, didn't come sit down with us, but stayed in the kitchen. He takes us to pretty spots, tells us about the problems the Chinese have now, that he had himself baptized Catholic, but that he really believes in Buddhism and in equality among people, freedom to think what you want to, and he whispers when he tells us of how he is forced to go to the Javanese police every month and give them some money, or else gangs will come and smash up his store. They talk softly about the serious matters of the day, and loudly, with a lot of chuckling, about before. They forget I'm there, don't need me and don't notice when I've left the room, look up when I return, offer me a piece of *durian,* a fruit with a sharp odor, that he has broken for her, carving the soft milky colored contents out of the hard split outer shell, as one

199

would for a child, and hands her the moist pieces, hands full of the creamy fruit, drops on the table, pieces of the flesh of the fruit on their chins and cheeks. She licks her fingers clean, one by one, something I was forbidden to do when I was young, and talks while he slips the last piece between her lips, tells of her sisters, about Aunt Yossa, about you, Grandma, because he knew you all.

My mother had been very quiet and morose the first week, but then for three weeks was like Aunt Manda. She sang, she whistled when she walked and on the beach, because there was nobody besides us, she bared her upper body just like I did. I peered between my lashes at the way she surrendered to the sun on her skin, and how her body turned red, because she had obstinately refused the lotion with radiant outrage, "Are you crazy, I'm an Indies girl. I never used to put that stuff on either."

Then I thought: why did my father make every woman except my mother laugh?

"Don't say," she said on the plane on our way home, "that I saw my old boyfriend. He's very jealous, and then I'll have problems for months."

"There isn't anything wrong in seeing somebody again and talking to them, is there?" I had responded, irritated.

At which she said, her lips tight again like they were at home, "You don't know your father."

I think that Grandpa would have preferred to see a marriage between my mother and that Chinese man. But what had it changed? Hadn't she stood there in the kitchen with her back to the company, in the shabby dress that served as an apron at the same time, her hair greasy from hanging over the stove.

Grandma, I'm sure she felt the ribbon during those two days and as I was able to recognize the ribbon in her eyes, she also recognized it in mine.

There was a carnival and it was Saturday. I had looked myself over from all angles in my mother's full-length mirror before going out the door with Lotte. Aunt Eva had miscut a dress in sewing class, it didn't fit right under the arms, but you couldn't really tell, and she had given it to you along with some pedal-pushers when you saw her in Australia. I was the only one in the family the modern dress fit. My mother wouldn't let me go to school in it, but now, on my free afternoon, I was allowed to wear it because the seams ran a little crooked for Sunday and the fabric, a pink-and-white Brigitte Bardot-check, she thought was too shoddy for Sunday mass. I felt sunny in the dress, felt like skipping or dancing, my bare feet in the elegant sandals I had gotten as hand-me-downs from you. We already wore your size, you remember, Grandma, we always took your nicest new shoes home with us after staying with you.

At home my mother had cried, "What are you walking around bare-legged like that for? Put on your nylons or some knee socks, and watch how you're sitting, legs together, did you remember to put on a double pair of underpants?"

Peter was walking with the sales girl from the grocery, who was really supposed to be working, not hand-in-hand, but side-by-side, him with his hands in the pockets of his tight jeans, she moving her arms restlessly as she talked, and she talked a lot. He looked around.

From my monthly allowance I bought a stack of tickets for the whirligig, two dimes back, enough for two coffees from the vending machine at school, but nothing mattered to me any-more. I let my head drop back, my hair in the wind, pushed with my legs to go higher, to veer more wildly, and knew I was being watched by Peter.

When he picked me up from school, almost every day, I didn't say a word back when he talked, and to his questions I said hardly a yes or a no, because I thought it wasn't right to speak to strangers you didn't know from school, somebody who, on top of that, was dating somebody else. But now that he had been waiting for me for almost an entire school year, I did kind of want to go with him in the "doing eighty around the curve," lots of jolts, a lot of yelling, and maybe his arm around me, my head against his chest.

Lotte gave me a little sign, we still had exactly fifteen min-utes to be home right on time. She was waiting for me at the booth, was signaling furiously and smiling at Peter who was pointing up at me and there wasn't a trace of the girl to be seen anywhere.

I whirled up all my tickets. Lotte was stamping her feet, pointing at her watch, and acted as if she were preparing to go home. Reluctantly I undid the chain and slipped off the wooden seat.

"It's over," she shouted in my ear in order to be heard over the music of the rides, "he's stopped seeing her. He's free!"

He was talking to a boy, kicking his shoe against a broken car tire in rhythm to the music. I staggered, was dizzy, felt the ground move under my feet, didn't want to show that I was hoping he'd come over, turned around as resolutely as possible and motioned to Lotte, "You want to go?"

Lotte punched me, "Dummy," she said.

But I kept on walking. I felt light, I felt pretty and I was sure that he would follow. If that's being self-assured, Grandma, that feeling that nothing can go wrong, that you like yourself and therefore know for sure that he likes you too, then that was the only moment I was self-assured in my life.

He came after us near the police station. We were just rounding the corner, the fair far behind us, and there, he picked me up, swung me in the air, set me down carefully on the ground again after lots of rounds in the air, lay both his hands in my neck, his thumbs under my chin, and said, "Are you coming tonight! I broke up only for you."

It's so strange describing how it feels, feeling that you're floating, that you don't weigh a thing, that you're invisible, that you don't just feel the ribbon but that you've become the ribbon.

Lotte said, "We have to run, she'll give us hell!"

Out of breath we reached the back door at a quarter to six, three-quarters of an hour late. My mother was standing at the ready with her wooden spoon. First she beat Lotte, the way she usually beat Lotte first, because she's older and because Lotte provoked my mother into hitting her, sometimes hitting back or defending herself in such a way that my mother's rage grew rather than diminish at each blow. But it seemed as if she had seen the ribbon in my eyes, because she suddenly raised the wooden spoon toward my face and hit my cheeks, which she seldom did—she preferred our behinds—because there are brains in your head and they were sacred. Lotte shouted, "Go ahead, beat us, beat us, you're only jealous because you can't go to the carnival anymore yourself, beat us, it doesn't bother me, beat us to a pulp."

We weren't allowed out that evening, but we didn't want to go anyway because we were embarrassed about her, that she didn't realize that you can't beat girls of fourteen and fifteen as if they were children, and we didn't want Peter and his friends to see our welts and have to laugh about a mother who is jealous about being too old for the carnival.

XI

Just as I was getting to know her a little bit, she died.

Every woman in Asia, every girl twelve, fourteen, sixteen, twenty years old, every woman at a market with oranges, mangoes, bananas and *rambutan* spread out on the ground in front of her knees, every woman young, old, a porter along the highway with a pile of bricks on her head and a cloth in front of her mouth against the dust and exhaust fumes, a waitress, a farm laborer, a whore, makes me think of the two little portraits of the Javanese girl, sketched in pencil full-face and from the side, in a prewar wooden frame above my father's and mother's bed: my Grandma Melanie.

"Shall we lay a wager as to whether the cockatoo will take back its freedom or whether it'll stay with you because the jungle doesn't hold any interest for it since it gets his food and drink from you?"

"Well, what do you think?"

"You first."

"I don't like betting."

Neo always let me choose first, in everything, but made certain that we finally did what he had in mind all along.

I had no idea what Kasesa would want. According to the papers that went with the bird, it is just as old as you, Grandma, and originally comes from that area, probably from the Trobriand Islands, in fact.

I had started the book from which Martin, it seemed years ago, had read aloud to me to find out what Neo's plan entailed and I was really getting into it. The more I read about it, the clearer it became that it was a place to visit with Martin instead, because Martin likes those kinds of adventures, whereas Neo is really more accustomed to four-star hotels and organized package vacations.

"Say, Meisje," Neo said, "I hope you don't mind, but I didn't ask that cockatoo artist to come along because it seems to me it would be more fun just the two of us making that trip, with the bird, of course, as an accompanying alibi, than to have an old drunk like him along, because that man boozes, you've never seen anything like it, and then he gets incredibly aggressive, my God. . . to be saddled with company like that looking over your shoulder. . . I already told Martin that the artist is coming down later on, flying down on his own to Bangkok, where we have to stop over anyhow, because it seemed like a stroke of luck to be with you in Bangkok. I always wanted to see that city and you already know your way around so well. It'll be great to be shown the town by a woman. With Lieve I'm always the one who has to figure out what we're going to see and where we're going to go eat."

I started getting restless. At night I would toss and turn. At times I could have screamed with longing for Neo, imagined his hand, his mouth, on my body and I would push Martin away whenever he threw his arm around me. Then again I would decide never to see Neo again, because I couldn't look Martin straight in the eye.

We were sitting out in the back yard. It was hot, but still not summer. Martin and I had been talking about our son who hardly ever sent us news, who practically wasn't to be gotten hold of, when Neo strolled around the back of the house, whistling, and stood in front of us. He tossed the tickets triumphantly on the patio table and said, "Good afternoon, aren't you two sitting there all happy in your little yard, when behold: the trip of your dreams to the island of love. Tell me honestly, Martin, don't you think it's a shame that you can't come along? Everything's booked. Are you sure you don't want to postpone your dissertation a bit and fly down with us?"

Martin got up out of his lawn chair to fold out another one for Neo, turned his back on us, set up the chair, turned on both feet to face us again and said, "Why don't you two wait a couple of months? Meisje, if you come with me now, then I'll move up my departure date for Kalimantan, I'll shorten my research time and when I'm done with my work, Neo will fly, together with that artist, to Asia, and then the four of us can go to those islands."

Sometimes, Grandma, I don't understand a thing about myself. The night before I had hoped intensely that Martin would change his plans, that he would join us and that I wouldn't have to betray him, and now that he had proposed a plan I leapt out of my lawn chair and said, "I don't feel like going with you for that half-baked science that nobody gains anything from!"

Neo was taken aback. I could tell by his face that his sympathy for Martin was not a pretense.

Martin left the kitchen, went to his study and even though I couldn't hear it from outside, I was convinced he was sitting in front of his word processor.

"I'm going to go," said Neo, "I'll leave you two alone."

"If you do that, I won't go with you to the Trobriand Islands. You can't abandon me now."

"Who's abandoning whom right now?" Neo asked.

Our first fight.

I should have known, Grandma, that after the drive in the open car with *Vespers* in the background and the flat gray landscape of Flanders for a backdrop, the most ecstatic moment of my life because I'd never before known abandon as at that moment, in the back seat, my mouth and cheeks numbed by the wind that whipped my face, that punishment would follow.

Do you know, Grandma, that I felt guiltier in terms of Lieve than in terms of Martin? I kept thinking, what if Martin had been sitting in back with Lieve and me in front unsuspectingly with Neo, and then it tore at me inside. In those days I was drinking a lot of milk, got up a couple of times a night to heat up some milk and still I kept yearning to go on that trip alone with him.

At the same time I knew that it could only go wrong.

The night before we left I had the following dream: I was in the kitchen making *soto ayam,* my favorite dish. The chicken was already in the big pot—I was expecting a lot of guests. I had neatly prepared the ingredients in various pretty bowls, the *emping,* the *su-oon,* the boiled potatoes, the chopped vegetables, the fried onions, the hard-boiled eggs already peeled, the bouillon smelled good, and the *boómbu* that I'd pounded and fried with garlic and spices was already steeping in the soup. I greedily inhaled the smells rising from the pot, stirred the soup, prodded the chicken with the wooden spoon to see if it was cooked through yet, and discovered that I was fixing my own cockatoo.

We didn't get any farther than Bangkok. I was annoyed by

207

the way he looked at the girls, the young prostitutes, and that he didn't immediately understand that it was too painful when he said they were beautiful, smacking his lips, looking at them as if they were ripe mangoes. But particularly when he said he knew just what he would have done if he had been there by himself.

He thought I was jealous.

Jokes, he said, that was humor and it disappointed him that I didn't have a sense of humor, either, and that was his basic criticism of the female sex, that women couldn't laugh at themselves.

We quarreled like children, about everything, about nothing.

Why couldn't I just say, "It's as if you bought me, not with money, not with those tickets, but with your hands, your tongue, with your sensitivity to my body, by giving me the feeling that I'm special. I've become an object, I've become merchandise, already satisfied with a caress or a compliment, I evidently don't need payment, or even any proof that this might be real love, still less a promise that this possible love might last forever. . . ."

He turned the television on. The Thai news resounded in the room, while I lay on the bed and wrote:

A short poem.
He, his body stiff
in the only chair,
stares at the tube.
Snow and stripes.
Much interference.

He called home because he'd feel rotten if something should happen to him while Lieve thought he was in California on business. I could hear him from the bathroom, water running, the shower head aimed at Kasesa whom I'd put on a stool behind the shower curtain while I was holding onto the bird with one hand and spraying with the other, not knowing if I was aiming right because I had my ear pressed against the door.

"I had to go to Bangkok all of a sudden and I don't know how long it will take. Met some very interesting poets and artists. And I want to meet some of the rich people here, because there's quite a few of them, to open a new market. I don't know if it'll amount to anything. It's primarily an investment for the future. But it's important, now that things are only getting worse for us. We have to direct ourselves at other areas of the world. Of course. You know how awful it is for me to travel by myself. I miss you all very much. I'm sick with wanting my five sweet little girls. But I've tucked their pictures in the frame of the mirror. Sure, put them on. . . well, give me the littlest one first. . . my little Sweet Pea."

I forgot to mention the many women who have made me. We always think we've been made by our mothers and as an Indies girl you tacitly assume that you've been made by your grandmother and your aunts, maybe because, like your mother, they took care of you. But there are more women who have it on their consciences that I sometimes hate myself.

Women I met in the street every day when I was bicycling to school, with curlers in their hair, putting out the trash, women all made up and dressed in open dusters, with their white legs in slippers, who brought the construction workers coffee, shortly after which the men would go inside, one by one, the curtains closed. Women whom I've spent only an hour with in my life, but who have left an imprint behind in my soul, proof that it can also be different, that I don't have to tame myself.

I had only just become a mother and Martin had organized a meeting at our house, I don't remember what about anymore, because at that time we were trying to discuss so many things with others: shared housing groups, shared living arrangements, communes, housing projects, a living-working collective, all kinds of ways to find a solution to stifling the fear, the anxiety. I took part in these discussions, maybe I even had the biggest mouth, and at these meetings I was always enthusiastic about shared child care, sharing the use of the kitchen and the other practical advantages, but in bed at night I'd think about the shared bathrooms, the recurring group meals in a large kitchen at the same table and our possibly participating was out of the question again. One time at a meeting there was a woman, two years older than I, wearing a fetching summer dress, one leg up on a chair, her lips red, her eyes narrowing whenever a remark surprised her. Not paying attention to the conversation anymore, I observed her, a woman, and felt myself a girl, a child, clumsy, naive, the way I was sitting with my legs clamped together, my body cramped up on a wooden chair. Due to the smoke she exhaled nonchalantly across the table, over the empty cups and saucers dirtied by her tobacco, ashes and butts, I started coughing, my hands gripping the edges of my chair, as if I were sitting in a motorboat that was racing over the water, afraid of falling overboard. And I thought: I'm my own mother and she is Aunt Manda.

I won't ever forget her, her loud disarming laugh when she caught Martin at what she termed: his double standard.

She explained to him how he wanted to have all the advantages of living together with others, but none of the disadvantages. And I'll never forget how, holding her hand-rolled cigarette loosely between thumb and forefinger, she said, "If I'm allowed to cook for you, to baby-sit your son, then why shouldn't I, for example, because I think it's so delicious, which she does too, of course," at which she laid the hand with the cigarette on my knee and let it slide up my leg toward my crotch, "get together with your wife. . . say from eight to ten at night, while you all," at which she pointed with her cigarette at the other men at the table, "watch *Sports Round-Up,* and the both of us go and have a nice time in the shower."

The third grade teacher, in a great wide skirt with a petticoat, red spike heels, short ratted hair, glasses with heavy frames whenever she stood in front of the class, walked without her glasses on across the school yard, her hands behind her back, just like the two male teachers beside her, one on either side, whenever they walked around the yard. Only then could you see her laugh, when she was walking around gabbing with them, but sometimes she would suddenly run away from the two men toward a group of children and box them on the ears. Tap tap tap tap the tall spike heels hacked into the concrete tiles. Her skirt flounced up and down so that her petticoat became visible.

I even dreamed about her later when I was pregnant, nightmares, because as a child I had been scared of her. She was strict. Even when, like me, you really did your best at school, got good grades, she was unkind. She couldn't stand slowpokes, she said, and if you had been disobedient, slow or sleepy in class, she would punish you during sports.

We had to stand in two lines, facing each other, and make a long arch, she said, joining our hands in the air like a lean-to over the long corridor whose walls we formed. Through this she sent the culprit, the one with a failing grade, the kid with the black marks, and we were forced to kick and jeer at the child who was making its way through the corridor we formed, the harder and meaner the better. Any child who tried to back out of this was sent through afterward. I don't recall much now about her classes, but I do recollect every time she made us make that archway, and how I attempted fearfully to act as if I were kicking, carefully doing my best not to touch anybody and still trying to look as mean as possible.

If somebody had been bad, she'd pick a child out of the group that was fat, or somebody who'd forgotten their gym shoes, also once a girl who couldn't run fast, Téa her name was, white hair and transparent skin. Actually I thought the girl was nice, she learned poorly and I'd whisper the answers to dictations and arithmetic to her. She was slow, always seemed to be asleep and wasn't permitted by the others to play tag because she'd end up being It all recess. Téa stood still, at which the teacher made us stop being a corridor, but a circle instead, and she screamed, "What're you standing there for, let her have it. Or do you all want to be in the circle?"

I don't know if the others went home and told about what happened at school during sports class. I kept my mouth shut, thought it was supposed to be that way, even though I thought it was horrible and never forgot that teacher. For a long time I was still scared of red pumps, but a few years ago I bought some on purpose, because I thought it would help, things like that, something insignificant that makes you grow.

I can still smell the math teacher, in my mind a spinster of eighty, but she was probably fifty, unmarried—she lived with her sister who was sickly—who wore a suffocating perfume and had the face of an owl all covered with a thick layer of powder, her lips a harsh pink. That morning I'd left for school extra early, before my mother had gotten up, dressed for the first time in the miniskirt, that with my Grandma's help I'd cut from an old dress of Aunt Eva's, with the wide hem which Grandma objected to because it looked ugly, a wide hem like that, but which I kept wide so that at too much hassle from my mother I could drop the hem an inch or so. I wanted to get away from the boys' wolf whistles. That much attention I hadn't really expected. I went early to homeroom and did the math homework I'd forgotten to do. The classroom filled up. Some of the boys again started shouting out their praises for my new garment. And then she came in. Obviously she had already seen me in the hall or in the school yard. She called me to the front of the classroom but I didn't understand what was the matter. I stood next to her desk, thought she wanted to check my homework, my notebook in my hand, when she squatted down with a big pair of scissors that she had pulled out of her desk drawer and started cutting the threads loose, then she roughly tugged the hem so carefully ironed by my Grandma open and then down. After that she triumphantly sent me back to my seat.

From that moment on I skipped all her classes and later also the other one's so it would be less noticeable. I was better at math than at languages, but I dropped all the math classes and chose languages. I still greeted her in a friendly manner whenever I met her bicycling home from school and she was out walking her two little white dogs.

I know. I didn't write a thing about my other Grandma, with the same name as me, but according to my father she was really called Durga, and her father's family name was Charita, Durga Charita, the prettiest girl in the village when Marco Fleurie proposed to her.

"My father was disinherited because he marries her, because she is Javanese, and he is a white Indo, so they think he's ruining his chances. But my mother is very pretty and she can sing well. I believe that's how they got to know each other, because she sings, and he thinks: well, who is it with that beautiful voice. He is there only temporarily, he is sitting on his

213

porch, listening to the birds and the crickets and then he hears my mother, she is hauling well-water nearby, which is strange, because mostly the women don't do that when it's already evening. He gets curious and goes over to have a look. By chance she is there so late, I think her brother is sick, and of course she is startled by this man, that he is spying on her. She is accustomed to us Indos and Dutch people, because her father is the village elder, and she already knows what he wants, but she also knows that she can't do anything if he wants to do her harm, so that's why she sings, not in Javanese anymore, but in Pasar Malaysian, in those days they didn't speak Bahassa Indonesian like they do now, all those different peoples speak Pasar Malaysian to each other, and she sings, 'I am afraid that you want to harm me, you are strong and I am weak, what you want of me I cannot give you, but I see your eyes, beautiful and warm, and maybe you are sweet and therefore I won't run away from you, but will ask you, go to my father tomorrow, he is the *lurah,* and ask him for my hand.' Yes, her father is the *lurah,* that means village elder, so not just anybody, he commands respect, and that's the way it went. Otherwise, because it is that way in those days, my father might not recognize his limits, but now he has fallen in love, so he goes to her father and they marry. Or, well, marry, not right away. She had to take religion classes first, that's the law you know, and then she becomes Catholic or Protestant, Lord knows, all the same aren't they, then she is called Melanie, she gets a European name and then they get married."

My father's sisters said that their grandfather, whom they never knew, wasn't a village elder.

"Your father has quite an imagination," said Aunt Nun, a sister two years his senior. "My mother's father is not so high up, he is a storyteller, poor, really, he goes from village to village and tells tales, but also things that really happened, a walking newspaper you'd call a person like that here in Holland, maybe, I don't know for sure since my Dutch isn't so good because my mother has no money for our schooling. My father died young, you know. My grandfather, Pak Charita, is somebody that entertains people, because we can't read books of course."

In my parents' bedroom hang two drawings on yellowed paper, shoddily framed in a single wooden picture frame. At first glance the little portraits don't seem very significant. She looks like a girl with her open round face, the lips just barely shut, her eyes grave, her hair combed straight back, bare shoulders and a batik sarong bound tightly over her breasts. If you look well you can see the draftsman's love for each detail in her face, the highlights in her eyes, the slight dimple in her left cheek, a drop of sweat on the right near her temple. Very small, with the same pencil, in even handwriting is written, "My dear Melanie Durga Charita." And in the very corner of each of the drawings are the initials MF, bonded together the way I imitated the grandfather I never knew, beneath every poem, on every drawing.

"Too bad my father died so young, he can draw very well. Maybe I got it from him, except I don't have talent like he does. My mother used to have landscapes of his, and people at the market, a parrot on a branch, that kind of thing. I like them, but she sells them because he doesn't have any money, you know. Too bad, otherwise he is the Picasso of Java, if he is still alive."

To go visit her we first have to take buses, a train, and another bus, a lot of waiting on the way, and at her apartment there are lots of stairs. I am surprised that I reach her shoulder, think she is a midget, like my Aunt Yossa, but my father says not. Lotte goes outside again almost right away. She says she wants to jump rope, bugs me to come, but I don't want to, I stay. Later Lotte says she couldn't stand it because of the strange smell in that apartment and I understand what she means, but I, on the other hand, am fascinated by that smell, want to inhale it deeply.

At her place, for the first time we get the sweets that are wrapped in plastic and leaves. I'm already a lot older when we get those at Grandma Charlotte's too. The oil paintings of volcanic landscapes and rice fields that my father makes, but that my mother doesn't want to have up, are hanging all over the walls. I never knew where they were, thought they were kept in the back of his closet along with all kinds of stuff that my mother doesn't want to have in the living room or in the bedroom. Bright green, bright blue, and also a lot of orange, because of the setting sun, because the sun is usually setting in his paintings. She hasn't framed them, but tacked them up on the wall, here and there, with thumbtacks, also with nails that half stick out of the wall.

There is an uncle, but he isn't home when we are there. I have trouble calling her Grandma. I think it's because of the traditional Javanese sarong and *kebaya*, the bun in her neck, and because she speaks poor Dutch.

My mother is not there with us. My father says, when the little woman opens the door, "This is my mother, give her a kiss."

I say, "Hi, Grandma."

Lotte kisses her without a word.

(Lotte is happy that this Grandma never comes to our birthdays, because she would be ashamed, she says, what would those Dutch children think if they saw her.)

From behind the oil paintings and even wallpaper she pulls out bank notes. Five-guilder notes, but also some of larger denominations. My father is shocked.

She has been saving up to go back, she says, because she doesn't want to die here. Preferably there, near her father and her husband Marco.

We aren't to tell my father's brother, she says, because he won't understand, he hates Indonesia after what happened, but she still loves the country, her country, and my father has to help her, he knows the ropes in The Netherlands. All kinds of things she pulls out of batik cloths.

My father protests, "That money isn't enough, you know. And I already went through so much trouble to have you come here. My younger brother was wrong when he transferred to the Indonesian army while I'm telling him that he should go with us. There's enough work here, everything's quiet here, but he's headstrong, doesn't want to listen, till he writes me: please help me, I'm in trouble! And all that explaining I have to do, all those letters to the queen, and you've been here only two years now and you already want to go back. You won't die for a long time yet. Just try living here, first."

The other time I remember visiting her, my mother came along too. The uncle is also at home, so is his wife and a little baby. This aunt speaks no Dutch. The baby can't talk yet. My Grandma is sick. I think that's why we came, because most times my father goes by himself. When I think nobody's around and that she's asleep, I peek behind the oil paintings and behind the wallpaper to see if the bank notes are still there, but I don't see any. My mother washes the dishes, mops the kitchen floor, cleans the windows inside and wipes down the doors with a sponge and detergent. After that she cleans the little bathroom as well. Lotte and I escape outside because we're afraid that we'll have to help. On the train my mother complains to my father that they had just thrown the baby's dirty diapers into pails without rinsing them first. "That's where sicknesses come from," says my mother, "and they won't adapt, they still don't know how you're supposed to live in a country like The Netherlands."

My father remains silent. Most of the time he lets my mother do the talking. With words she always gains the upper hand over my father, and he gains the upper hand over his mother and his younger brother, but his brother speaks better Dutch than his mother and his wife, so that's why he decides what's going to happen where they're concerned. (That's what I saw when I was ten, or eleven, I don't remember anymore exactly, maybe I was younger, and I whispered to Lotte one night in our small double bed, "The one who speaks the best is the boss."

Lotte agreed. "That's why I always get A's for Dutch," she said, "the rest doesn't matter to me.")

She is in the hospital. My father has given Lotte and me some small change for fries. That has never happened before, and after that, never again, because even our monthly allowance he gives us reluctantly and tries to skip altogether, or he'll say, "Go ask your mother, I don't have anything." He never gives us money the way Uncle Didi or the other uncles often give their children if there's something to celebrate, or just for the heck of it, and then we'll get a dime too, when they get two. But now my father is giving us money, and I can still see the coin in my hand, am conscious of how I stare at it, incredulous. And we don't have to hurry, he says, as long as we don't wander off.

We eat the last of our fries in the hospital corridor, and then they're suddenly stern: we have to hurry up, no dillydallying, no touching our coats with our mayonnaise fingers, no talking so loud, and as fast as we can go down the stairs and outside. In an unfamiliar car, with an aunt we don't know very well yet, we drive to Grandma's house. A short while later Grandma is suddenly home, brought by an ambulance. We stand on the balcony and watch as it drives up, but have to wait indoors, otherwise we'll be in the way, and because we don't have the time anymore to take off our winter coats and scarves in the hall, it is hot in the tiny living room, the heater turned up, where we sit squeezed up against unfamiliar cousins on the sofa with sweet, gooey, pastel-colored candies wrapped in clear plastic in our hands, mittens dangling on strings from our sleeves.

We stand around her bed. She wanted to die in her own bed and if we didn't listen, she would come and haunt us because in that hospital with all those strangers her soul would find no peace. Extreme unction she had refused because that had been thought up by humans. Aunt Nun's oldest son explains everything, whispering in my ear. He understands Javanese and Indonesian because he was born on Java and went to school there and he had Javanese-speaking friends there, he says. He is fourteen, is named Werner and at the snack bar he gave me extra money for a hot dog and some salad.

Suddenly Aunt Nun starts to cry very noisily, she lies down on my Grandma and shakes her mother roughly, "Don't die, don't die."

Grandma says, "*Suratan tangan.*" Then she dies, I can see it, Werner doesn't have to tell me that.

Later, on the train, my parents quarrel about what she said.

Grandma's last words, says my mother, were, "The will of God be done." My father becomes furious. He makes a move with his arm as if he wants to hit her, a gesture I have never seen him make. I have never seen him this angry. Lotte and I look around to see if the other passengers have noticed his anger.

"What do you know about that language? You can only say

if I believe is spelled E before I or not. *Suratan tangan* has nothing to do with God."

"What then, what do you think it means?" My mother's expression belies a challenge.

"Your fate is determined, it means, that's what it means, your fate is determined."

"So, what did I say," chafes my mother's voice, "it's the same thing."

"It isn't the same at all, that mumbo jumbo about God, she didn't say that at all."

"Your fate is determined, that's exactly the same as the will of God be done, see, that's how you say it."

"What do you know about it? My mother says nothing at all about God. She means something entirely different. You always think you know everything."

"Yes, of course I say I know, because I know that those two things mean the same thing."

"What do you know about it? She's *my* mother."

As a child I shouted so many times, "What are you two doing together? Go and get divorced if you always argue!"

They argue the whole way, outside it is dark, black behind the glass in which we are reflected. My brothers sleep on his and her laps, accustomed to their quarrelsome voices. Only the oldest one looks up when my father trembles with rage.

In the smoky terminal of the bus station where we wait for the last bus to our village while it's freezing outside and with every gust of wind snow blows in, they start up again. My mother attempts, "If you say that God willed it that way, then you really mean to say that your fate is determined by God,

220

that you have to accept that life takes its own course."

He shouts, and undoubtedly doesn't know what he's saying anymore. His entire body expresses loathing for every word still coming out of my mother's mouth, and his whole comportment is aimed at deflecting each thing she says, making it clear to her that she has to be quiet. The other people in the terminal look up with a start when his voice resounds with desperate fury through the crowded station, "God didn't determine anything at all. You're being a nag."

I whisper to Lotte, "I know what it means. Werner translated it for me. It just means, 'It is written in my hand.'"

To Martin I said, "Neo got scared at his very first confrontation with public transportation. He has an exaggeratedly romantic idea of places like that, and wants to maintain it. He can't take reality." I also lied and told him that the Flemish artist had called the hotel in Bangkok to say he didn't want to come, that everything had been arranged for the sake of the special edition, so what was the sense in taking the trip if the artist wasn't coming and that on top of it all, traveling with Kasesa had been a disappointment, because the cockatoo had caused too many delays in spite of the special permits and papers and that it was dead tiring to be on the road with a bird.

"I knew that all along," said Martin.

XII

Many beautiful moments I have forgotten. I can still remember that it was great at some time or other, but I can't remember why. Pain I remember longer. Also the why.

You have to forget, to be able to be a child again.

I can see myself lying down, waiting, my focus on infinity, listening to the sounds passing by and enjoying the cold wind caressing my nakedness.

Actually I wanted to write a book, but instead I wrote a letter you will never read, but if you should read it you will listen to the sound of each word, and there won't be any meaning. There is too little time for you to play with the previous sentences.

You sit in front of the television, watch the news and say to Aunt Yossa, "Just look at this, those men, always fighting. Why? you ask yourself."

When Grandpa told me, "I sinned, I abandoned my wife and children for a foolish infatuation and now I have to pay for that, that's why, I know. . . ," I asked you, away from the others, "Grandma, when Grandpa went off with that young girl, were you able to forgive him?"

"Forgive, yes," you said, with that mysterious glow in your face, "but forget, never of course."

On your ninetieth birthday I tried again, "Grandma, for how long did Grandpa leave you?"

"With which girl, what do you mean? Who left?"

"Grandpa! For how long did Grandpa leave you?"

"Grandpa? Do you mean my grandfather? I never really knew him. On either side."

"No, your husband, *my* grandfather."

"But my husband's been dead a long time."

"But when he was still alive, for how long did he leave you? That time in Indonesia when he left for a while. How long was it?"

"Well I'll be. If you ask me, I don't even remember that he left."

Of the, I believe, eighty women who came to my fortieth birthday party there isn't one whom I'd dare have read this letter. I don't even dare give this letter to Lotte.

Of course not to Aunt Manda, but maybe to Aunt Yossa. . . .

It is strange to realize that you don't really dare to show anybody who you are. Women have always fascinated me more than men. When I was little I already preferred to look at women's bodies, but that disappeared and made way for the need to talk with women, to know how they think, to see the little lights in their eyes. More and more admiration grew for women who independently fought their way through life, who didn't seem to need men. Elsa will shortly be celebrating her sixtieth birthday, but everybody thinks she isn't even fifty, the way she stirs up the people in the audience from the stage or makes them quiet as mice with her sometimes raw, sometimes tantalizing voice. Helena, who makes intriguing documentaries and always keeps coming up with something whose existence is still unknown to viewers, so that they, badgered by her images, would like to do something immediately about the problem that she dishes up for them in fifty minutes. Louise, a quiet but strong woman, a pianist who would like nothing better than have young girls get acquainted with her instrument so they won't give up playing after only two years, but will continue, and the pride with which she attends her ex-students' concerts is moving. Then there's Wendy, who knows how to be exceptionally self-effacing when it comes to letting her husband, a well-known television personality, receive all the praise, but who is her husband's backbone. Then there's also Hetty, a country girl, a farmer's daughter without any education, younger than I am, who used to let herself be beaten by her husband, but who stood up to his physical dominance, dragged him to a therapist, and who fought for her love, so that they were now at my party beaming, hand-in-hand, while their grown son shuffles across the dance floor with his first girlfriend. She started her own business, independently of him and thereby compelled him to respect her. She has forgotten that he used to beat her. I was so stupid to start up about it and she laughed, "That really was a long time ago. It's only because you bring it up, but otherwise I really wouldn't remember anymore."

Men have another effect on me. I'm spoiled by my being different, feeling people's eyes. But with boys my own age and later with men of all ages, I wanted to check the motive for their looks. I wanted to have some kind of proof that the reason for their attention was one of respect or admiration, I wanted their laughter, but I particularly wanted to be their equal. I was always seeking balance and it upset me when it seemed as if the love wasn't equal. Because I like men, all men, even if they only deliver bread to the door, or sweep the chimney. Not to make love to, Grandma, but just like that, the way they put one foot in front of the other, their clumsiness, the hormones that roll off their tongues while they're talking, or which they attempt to conceal by being modest and polite, their buttocks clenched and their hands straight against their sides, their gruff voices, their red eyes, the I-don't-see-you look that sees that which doesn't want to be seen, the rude shout that disrupts their own voice, the downcast eyes and the penetrating stare, they make me a woman and remind me that it's wonderful to be a woman.

During the flight back home from Bangkok—after a lot of arguments full of reproaches we took the same plane back anyway—snuggled against one another, refused the in-flight meals and slept like brother and sister, like cousins, in each other's arms. I woke up with a feeling of pins and needles in my legs where the circulation seemed to have stopped, but didn't want to shift my position, knew that this was true love, because nothing was over, something had started, I thought.

He cried just before we landed, his head in my lap. The last time we'd be together, we had agreed.

Our baggage came out quickly. We had notified Martin, who was waiting for us. Kasesa had been boarded separately and that took time, waiting for that bird, so Neo said he figured he should be getting on his way, it was still a long drive to Flanders.

In the days that followed I called him every day for a few minutes. We didn't say much except how are things going, are things a little better, I miss you and I miss you too.

It was over, I had said and he had concurred, that was all. It happened just like I had foreseen when he took the photo with the self-timer. My resisting hadn't helped. I had been photographed with temples before and didn't want to pose. But he had wanted a souvenir and that was the day we arrived, when we were still cheerful, passionately in love, despite the doubts that were already festering in him and in me; was this right, wasn't it sinful, weren't we going too far. . . .

As a surprise, Lieve had taken the film to be developed when she emptied the pockets of his jeans and had also picked up the pictures at the photo shop an hour or two later when she had finished her errands at the fish shop, the supermarket and the baker's and had, curious to see a part of the world she had never been to before, looked at the pictures in the shop.

"She's threatening divorce," he said, "and I'll die if I can't see my five daughters but once a month."

I couldn't eat anymore, sleep anymore. I spent the days in bed and at night I roamed the house, reread his letters, wrote poems, wrote letters to him that I would rip up, hundreds of pieces that I buried way down in the garbage.

Martin asked, "Hasn't Neo gotten in touch at all?"

I lied, "In the end he turned out to be really angry that we didn't go to the Trobriand Islands."

Our son said, "You two should have a second child, it'll do you good, then you'll feel young again." (He had his own diagnosis.)

Sometimes he would call and seem to be crying, his voice filled with despair, "I'm going crazy not seeing you anymore." Or four days later, "I want you, I miss you," after which we remained silent.

I didn't want to wait for his lines. I wanted to escape from the addiction of having to hear through the telephone that I existed.

Actually I wanted to die, but at the same time I thought it ridiculous to want to die over a man you don't love as much as your own husband. I hated myself, a deep hatred, Grandma, revulsion, I don't know how to tell you, I detested myself and my own wishes, I hated myself for not being able to surrender myself to Martin and couldn't understand why I wormed out of his embrace whenever he took me in his arms.

According to Helena you don't need to have sex so badly after menopause. Elsa says that since she turned forty she only had sex twice and that she isn't going to make a third attempt. Louise, who is forty-nine, has a lot of pain in her stomach and vagina, she says, which has been going on for almost a year, and luckily has her partner—who lives in another province—besides a couple of other steady contacts so that she doesn't feel guilty. Wendy has already not had her period twice, she says, and thinks sex is just a bother, even though her husband likes to have it two to three times a week, but, she says with a smile, "There are other ways to surprise one another."

I asked them all, Grandma, all the women as old as I am or older, because Helena scared me at my party when she said derisively, slightly drunk, with her back to the coat closet, a vodka on the rocks in her hand, "Enjoy it now, because in seven years it'll all be over, then they won't want you anymore but then you're happy yourself that they don't need you so bad."

I didn't feel like talking, only wanted to dance that night, but couldn't avoid a conversation without being rude. As an escape I stopped some woman who was walking by, a woman of about sixty, I guess, whom I didn't really know but who had come with my publisher, "What do you think about that?

Does our interest in sex change the older we get?"

"For me it's just starting," the lady responded, she theatrically ran her fingers through her short gray hair and winked. There was some giggling. A little crowd started gathering. "Nice discussion group," Lotte laughed. She stood still and pinched my arm.

Francien, a beautiful woman with red hair, dyed, because she's really gray but had been a dark blond, with big gray eyes, a little lipstick on her lips, a slender boyish body, and a small sparing mouth, forty-two, slightly drunk from three glasses of champagne, said loudly, "We haven't had sex in three months, he's always tired, and if I start caressing him he falls asleep."

Saskia, just thirty, sculptor and recent mother, spontaneously threw out, "Well, then I'd dump him."

"But I love the man," said Francien, "and we have three little kids."

"So take a lover," advised Saskia, and she pointed at one of the men on the dance floor who wasn't dancing but stood watching the band, hands in his pockets.

Francien snickered with her hand in front of her mouth, grabbed a fresh glass from the tray Lotte was taking around and said, "Yeah, he's a hunk, but I really like mine, I'll give him another try first."

Sounds of raucous laughter. Francien was laughing the hardest, I think, and gasped through it, "But it really isn't a laughing matter, you know. In bed I cry about it."

Helena stood and stared seriously. Even though Louise, Elsa, Wendy and the others were filled with hilarity, her gaze was unmoving and she said, "You get used to everything, even being forgotten, you get used to forgetting, because I didn't know that you could forget what it is to be a mother, but since my daughter's death, now the pain of the loss has faded, I can't remember what it was like to be a mother, either."

The others weren't listening, I was, and then I walked away to dance.

Over the phone Neo said, "Just try to imagine that you and I are unsuspectingly sitting in the front of that Caddy and Martin is meanwhile fingering my wife."

"I already thought of that."

"Well, what would you do if you turned around and suddenly realized what was happening, just imagine!"

"They didn't figure it out. There was nothing to be seen."

"That's not the point. Tell me honestly. What would you do?"

"So what would you do?"

"Sorry, you'll excuse me, my sweet, but I'd kill Martin."

"What hysteria," I said, "and what nonsense. As if Martin would, you know, your wife. . . ."

"Now wait a second, I'll put it a different way: We're married and I see you in the back with some guy, having a little. . . . I don't need any proof, you know. If I'd see him just with his hands under that blanket, I'd split his skull. I'd grab him by the neck and strangle him on the spot."

"Don't exaggerate so."

"You, too, Meisje, you can't handle something like that. You'd do the same thing."

"You don't know me," I said, and I can see myself jumping out of a moving pink Cadillac with the top down, bouncing along the road, bouncing like a ball, until a truck smashes me.

I didn't want to wait anymore for him to call, write or, which was very unlikely, show up at the door suddenly.

I opened up the atlas to a page at random, closed my eyes,

circled above the map with my finger and brought it down somewhere: Budapest.

There, on the street, by chance, I got to know a woman who was a literary agent. I had picked up a little book from the previous century for little money and listless with emptiness I fondled the worn leather cover like a frail memory of myself while I sat on a windy terrace with tea and a salty pastry, flipped through the small brown-tinged copy, inspected the minuscule etchings. She came and stood next to me, said she was the director of a publishing company and was fascinated by the little book in my hands, asked if she might see it for a moment.

She took me everywhere and said she thought it was fun to take a young woman to places where she herself, because she was fifty, didn't go anymore and then I didn't dare say that we only differed ten years in age. Maybe I behaved like a child by telling her that I was on the run, that I had left to forget somebody who was married with lots of children and kept silent about myself being a mother, with a husband who had asked me with concern to call every evening, because he had heard wild stories about women alone in Budapest.

Through her I got to know a lot of writers, especially men, because the women were all busy with family, housekeeping, alongside their careers as writers, and she was also the one who introduced me to the young poet who had just been published by her, a slim pretty young man my son's age.

(I quell my hunger with a new hunger, greedily, a new face, young eyes that make my languid old body become a girl's again.)

. . .

230

Aunt Manda said, "I do like a little bit of. . . uh. . . joking around. . . and such. . . but I always said to myself: To this point and no further."

Aunt Yossa waited in vain for a man to overstep his limits once.

I imagined a limit and saw myself keep shifting it.

He read aloud to me from his collection and translated everything, saw in my eyes whether I understood his explanation and kept looking for words to tell me not only the words but also the symbolism, and to have me recognize the sounds so that I would understand his rhyme. I thought I was in love again, but it was only the eagerness with which his eyes were constantly directed at me day in day out and during the long nights. After meeting, we had sat and talked for hours, shouted actually, to be able to hear one another over the Hungarian pop group and while we were talking I thought: he has to be older, he doesn't talk like a boy. He thought the same thing, he said afterward, that I was older than he thought from what I said, but that age was only digits in a passport, nothing more.

Suddenly, on the street I wake up out of his grasp. He and I find ourselves, happen to be somewhere outside, in the middle of the city, among piled-up tables and chairs where a few hours earlier people had still been eating goulash and pizzas, but where it is quiet now, because it is four, five o'clock in the morning.

"Don't you have any condoms?" I ask, because I'm almost sure that he can't have any and I want time to think.

He has them at home, he says, at his apartment, it's better to go there anyway.

"I'm expecting a phone call tomorrow morning, very early," I say, "I can't come over," which is true, because Neo was supposed to call, Martin had told me that morning over the phone.

"Shall I go with you to your place?"

"Out of the question," I say, "having visitors is forbidden in my hotel."

His face, the childish expression, the hungry look, makes me think of *Kanchil,* the little fairy tale deer, about which my father used to tell us before we went to sleep.

I kiss him like a mother, but he bites me, my cheeks, my neck, my shoulder. His teeth are everywhere.

He helps me forget Neo and he helps me go back to Martin.

I forgot what I felt.

(It's not my mother's Jiminy Cricket. I myself fold my wings back and decide not to fly. I don't want repetition whose outcome I already know.)

He pouts, is a child, talks like a man to win me over and says (full of reproach), "You give up on living."

I hold my tongue, see him standing there, his hungry mouth and say (feeling sorry), "Like you are, that's how I used to be."

When he calls, I say, "How's it going? Have you written anything?"

Then he says, in his sensual voice, his pleasant accent, "You sound like my mother, Melanie."

He taught me how to live again, Grandma, but the funny thing was that he brought me to the airport and thought I had decided to be dead for the most part.

Through him I knew that longing didn't stop at the one man I had gotten to know through Kasesa.

Martin picked me up, even though I had said that I would manage to get home by myself. But I was glad to see him, had longed for him, which hadn't happened in so long, or maybe it had, yes, in Bangkok, when I wasn't prepared to tell Neo why I found his jokes to be in poor taste, I had longed for Martin then, but especially his words, his explanation for what I myself was feeling and now I smelled his body, felt his stomach, his waist, thinner, at which he said that he hadn't eaten because he had missed me and we stayed in the car for a long time, our noses touching, his fingers on my lips, until Martin said, "At home we've got a nice soft bed."

And during the drive, his hand on my leg, my hand in his neck, he said, "Don't be alarmed, but Kasesa pulled out a few feathers, they evidently do that when they're lonely. I did my best, but the poor thing missed you, I believe."

Our child is visiting. He has brought two garbage bags full of dirty laundry, but always takes care of that himself. He has been dealing with the washing machine and the dryer since he was a boy of twelve, always understood that he shouldn't bother me when I was writing in my room.

Now, however, he comes into my workroom jubilant as a child, his voice high, his touching man's body forgotten for an instant, to where I am writing you, Grandma, now at this moment, and says in happy surprise, "Your cockatoo can so talk, I just heard it."

Because I don't react, he pulls me up from my chair. "Come on, come listen, it really talks, it talks."

I smile, Grandma, I nod, I don't feel like getting up, but he pulls me along again, "Really! It talks! It says, 'I love you.'"

She sits in front of the window. They invited her for a reading. She will be picked up and brought back so that the traveling won't tire her and she only has to read for a few minutes from her own work. A manuscript she couldn't get through herself anymore.

Her son will find it in her trunks, when he is looking for poems that he, for the first time in her life, will publish. On his deathbed his father asked him to do this. In sifting through the many drawers and antique chests he won't be able to find anything. But in the large trunk with the padlock that he impatiently forces with a chisel and a crowbar, the only tools around, he finds, in the cellar, hidden beneath forty years of old discarded carpeting, papers, folders, notebooks, diaries, poems, essays by his mother ever since she learned how to write at school. Practically on top he finds the manuscript—moisture has stained the paper green and gray—with the title: Letter to Grandma. It is written by hand. Some of the sections have been made all but unreadable by the mold. The date shocks him, he forgets that he is looking for her poetry, flips through it, reads fragments, and drops to the damp floor where he is captivated by the text from A to Z, except for the weathered, indecipherable portions.

"Meisje," because strangely enough he still calls her Meisje, after all she hasn't responded to Melanie for some time, "can you remember that you wrote a letter to Grandma?"

"What did you say, son?"

"Does it ring a bell, 'Letter to Grandma,' do you remember when you wrote that?"

"A letter to Grandma? I never wrote a letter to Grandma. My grandmother, both my grandmothers, died a long time ago. Which grandmother do you mean?"

"Do you remember writing a book that's called 'Letter to Grandma'?"

"The books I wrote are all there, son, on that shelf. I myself don't remember the titles of all the things I wrote."

He shows her the manuscript. She looks at it. She spells the title with difficulty. She complains, "What terrible handwriting."

"Meisje, I read it. Did what's written in that letter all really happen?"

She shakes her head. "That book isn't mine. I never wrote by hand. I always wrote on the word processor." And she turns away from him. "Look, look how beautiful." She points at the sunlight that, as every morning at that hour, slants in through the window, a ray of sunlight that falls on her brown-gray book and she reaches out her hand toward the dust particles dancing in the light. "Little sunspots." She lets the beam fall into her hand and says, "So funny, the way those little specks of light dance on the lines of my hand."

Glossary of Terms

Adú! Exclamation of pain (regret, yearning, envy, fright)

Alang alang Tall underbrush, prairie grass

Awas! Watch out, be careful

Ayó! Hurry up

Bahasa Language; language of Indonesia is Bahasa Indonesian

Belanda European

Boómbu Spices in general

Chabé rawit Small very hot pepper

Die Eltern (Our) Parents (*German*)

Dokar Horse-drawn trap with a roof but no sides

Doókoon Healer, shaman

Durian Large green fruit with small spines, creamy, with very strong odor

Eins mal drei macht drei, zwei mal drei macht sechs, dreimal drei macht neun One times three equals three, two times three equals six, three times three equals nine (*German*)

Eins, zwei, drei One, two, three (*German*)

Emping Spice

Ganz gewiss Certainly, that's true, of course (*German*)

Ikat Javanese twice-woven tie-dyed fabric

Indies, Indo Both terms have been used here to describe Indo(nesian)-Europeans, or rather Dutch-Indonesians; the former as feminine and cultural adjective, the latter to refer to Dutch-Indonesian males

Jambu Pear-shaped fruit with pit

Kampong Village compound

Kassian! Exclamation of pity for/over something

Kebaya White lace blouse with long fitted sleeves, worn by both women and men

Kelepon Grater used to grate cane sugar

Kenari Like an oversized walnut, a soft shell around a hard shell, white meat

Kroópook Shrimp shell flakes fried in deep fat to puff up like crackers and be eaten with a meal

Lieve Beloved, dear, kind (*Dutch*)

Lumpia Indonesian egg roll

Lurah Village leader

Mandi-tubs Bathing tubs

Meisje Girl (*Dutch*)

Nasi goreng Fried rice

Nasi kuning Yellow (turmeric) rice

Pasar Malaysian Malaysian spoken in urban areas in Indonesia and internationally

Rambutan Fruit

Rampokkers Indonesian gangs

Rujak Strong spices mixed with palm oil in a mortar and pestle into a pate which is used as a dipping sauce for unripe fruit

Salak Small apricot-sized fruit with brown snakeskin-like exterior, pale yellow flesh around a hard brown pit

Sapulidi Palm fiber broom

Saté kambing Goat kebab

Sik Beard

Slendang Sling to carry a baby

Soto ayam Chicken

Spekkoek Bacon-cake, named for the alternating thin brown and white pancakelike layers that make up this round, allspice-flavored Indonesian delicacy that takes hours to make (*Dutch*)

Su-oon Spice

Suratan tangan It is written in the palm of one's hand

Surat lepas Letter of divorce, as in Islamic code

Terasie Dried fish cake used as spice

Tikar Braided rattan or bamboo sleeping mat made to be rolled up

Tuar! Bingo!

Yang kechil The little one

About the Author

Marion Bloem was born in Arnhem in 1952, to East Indian parents who had moved to The Netherlands two years earlier. In addition to many publications including children's books, short stories, a collection of travel writing and six novels, of which *The Cockatoo's Lie* is the most recent, Ms. Bloem is also a filmmaker and artist.

In 1993 she was a writer in residence at the University of Iowa's International Writing Program.

About the Translator

After graduating as the first candidate of the Translation Program at the University of Iowa, Wanda Boeke received a Fulbright-Hays grant and continued to pursue literary translation in The Netherlands, France and Spain, working with a variety of novelists, poets and filmmakers there. She returned to Iowa in 1990 to join the staff of the International Writing Program, where she worked for two years as the Program's translation coordinator.

The Cockatoo's Lie is the translator's second novel to be published in the U.S. (Women in Translation published her translation of Renate Dorrestein's novel *Unnatural Mothers* in 1994.) Wanda continues with her commitment to introduce Netherlandic writers to American readers.

Welcome to the World of International Women's Writing

Unnatural Mothers by Renate Dorrestein. $11.95. ISBN: 1-879679-06-X
A compelling Dutch novel, by turns hilarious and heartbreaking, *Unnatural Mothers* explores the oldest bond in the world: that of mother and daughter.

The Four Winds by Gerd Brantenberg. $12.95. ISBN: 1-879679-05-1
This bittersweet coming-of-age novel, from Norway's leading feminist author, beautifully evokes a young woman's struggle to establish her identity as a scholar, a lesbian and a writer.

An Everyday Story: Norwegian Women's Fiction edited by Katherine Hanson. $14.95. ISBN:1-879679-07-8
Norway's tradition of storytelling comes alive in this enthralling anthology. The new expanded edition includes stories by contemporary writers, reflecting recent changes in Norwegian society: immigration, the artistic and cultural renaissance of the Sami and changing family structures.

Under Observation by Amalie Skram. With an introduction by Elaine Showalter. $15.95. ISBN: 1-879679-03-5
This riveting story of a woman painter confined against her will in a Copenhagen asylum is a classic of nineteenth century Norwegian literature by the author of *Constance Ring* and *Betrayed.*

Two Women in One by Nawal el-Saadawi. $9.95. ISBN: 1-879679-01-9
One of this Egyptian feminist's most important novels, *Two Women in One* tells the story of Bahiah Shaheen, a well-behaved Cairo medical student—and her other side: rebellious, political and artistic.

Unmapped Territories: New Women's Fiction from Japan edited by Yukiko Tanaka. $10.95. ISBN: 1-879679-00-0
These stunning new stories by well-known and emerging writers chart a world of vanishing social and physical landmarks in a Japan both strange and familiar. With an insightful introduction by Tanaka on the literature and culture of the "era of women" in Japan.

Wild Card by Assumpta Margenat. $8.95. ISBN: 1-879679-04-3
This lively mystery is set in Andorra, a kingdom between France and Spain. *Wild Card* tells the story of Rocio, a young sharp-witted woman who devises a scheme to beat her sexist boss at his own game.

How Many Miles to Babylon by Doris Gercke. $8.95. ISBN: 1-879679-02-7
Hamburg police detective Bella Block thinks she'll find some rest on her countryside vacation, but after only a few hours in the remote village of Roosbach, she realizes she has stumbled on to one of the most troubling cases of her career.

Originally established in 1984 as an imprint of Seal Press, Women in Translation is now a nonprofit publishing company, dedicated to making women's writing from around the world available in English translation. We specialize in anthologies, mysteries and literary fiction. The books above may be ordered from us at 3131 Western Avenue, Suite 410, Seattle, WA 98121 (Please include $3.00 for postage and handling). Write to us for a free catalog.